Color and Mastering for Digital Cinema

Color and Mastering for Digital Cinema

Glenn Kennel

Digital Cinema Industry Handbook Series

Charles S. Swartz

ELSEVIER

AMSTERDAM • BOSTON • HEIDELBERG • LONDON
NEW YORK • OXFORD • PARIS • SAN DIEGO
SAN FRANCISCO • SINGAPORE • SYDNEY • TOKYO
Focal Press Is an Imprint of Elsevier

Cover photograph: Standard Evaluation Material (StEM) picture by permission of the American Society of Cinematographers (ASC) and Digital Cinema Initiatives (DCI). Color Timing Theatre is courtesy of Laser Pacific Media Corporation.

Acquisitions Editor: Angelina Ward
Series Editor: Charles S. Swartz
Technical Editor: Sarah Priestnall
Project Manager: Paul Gottehrer
Assistant Editor: Doug Shults
Marketing Manager: Christine Degon Veroulis
Cover Design: Alisa Andreola
Interior Design: Isabella Piestrzynska

Focal Press is an imprint of Elsevier
30 Corporate Drive, Suite 400, Burlington, MA 01803, USA
Linacre House, Jordan Hill, Oxford OX2 8DP, UK

 Recognizing the importance of preserving what has been written, Elsevier prints its books on acid-free paper whenever possible.

Library of Congress Cataloging-in-Publication Data
Application submitted

British Library Cataloguing-in-Publication Data
A catalogue record for this book is available from the British Library.

ISBN 13: 978-0-240-80874-1
ISBN 10: 0-240-80874-6

For information on all Focal Press publications
visit our website at www.books.elsevier.com

06 07 08 09 10   10 9 8 7 6 5 4 3 2 1

Printed in Canada

To Sarah and Lucy

Contents

Preface

The standardization of 35 mm film nearly 100 years ago paved the way for the growth of the motion picture industry. From its humble roots in nickelodeons and peep shows, the motion picture business evolved into popular entertainment for the masses. Along the way, the 35 mm film standard was extended to support sound, color, wide screen presentation, and multi-channel digital soundtracks.

The film-making process is being revolutionized by the adoption of digital imaging technologies. Digital post production was widely embraced in the 1990s, and digital cinema distribution and exhibition is now taking off with a consensus standard supported by all of the major studios.

This book describes the color mastering and encoding methods for digital cinema, looking back at the traditional film process, providing insight into the evolving digital intermediate process, and reviewing the basis for the color encoding standards for digital cinema distribution. One can only hope that these digital cinema standards can be as capable and enduring as 35 mm film.

Acknowledgments

I could not have written this book without the help of many people. First, I'd like to thank my wife, Sarah Priestnall, for checking my writing and correcting my mistakes, and also for helping me re-write sections for clarity, particularly the chapter on Digital Intermediate. I also thank her for her support and patience while I was spending many weekends on the writing.

I am deeply indebted to Tom Maier of Kodak for his lucid writing on the subject of color processing for digital cinema. In particular, much of Chapters 3, 4, 7, and 8 are based on documents that he wrote as a leading contributor to the SMPTE DC28 Color ad hoc group.

I also thank Matt Cowan of Real D for his contributions as a member of the SMPTE DC28 Color ad hoc group, and for his help in reviewing and editing the chapter on Digital 3D. Matt also contributed several illustrations to this book.

Brad Walker of Texas Instruments taught me a lot about the color processing that he designed for the DLP Cinema® projectors, and much of Chapter 9 is based on a paper that he co-authored with Greg Pettitt, also of Texas Instruments. Brad was also a key contributor to the SMPTE DC28 Color ad hoc group.

I'd also like to thank the other members of the SMPTE DC28 Color ad hoc group, who dedicated many hours to our discussions and evaluations leading up to the specification of X'Y'Z' color encoding for digital cinema distribution. This group also included Prinyar Boon, Chuck Harrison, Jim Houston, George Joblove, Howard Lukk, Arjun Ramamurthy, Jeremy Selan, John Silva, Kaz Tsujikawa, and Ron Williams.

I'd like to thank industry consultant Peter Putman for his contributions to Chapter 10 on Digital Display Technologies. Many of the illustrations in this chapter come from his tutorials to HPA and NAB audiences.

And finally, I'd like to pay a special tribute to Walt Ordway, Howard Lukk, and Jim Whittlesey of Digital Cinema Initiatives, who drafted the DCI System Specifications, and in the process built a technical and political consensus amongst the major studios, enabling the deployment of digital cinema.

About the Author

Glenn Kennel has worked in technology development in the motion picture industry for over 25 years, pioneering the application of digital technology to the filmmaking process He started his career with Eastman Kodak in 1980, and participated in the development of Kodak High Speed Negative Film 5293.

In the mid-1980s, Kennel assembled a project team and led the development of a prototype HDTV telecine that later provided the basis for the Philips Spirit Datacine. In 1989, he worked with Industrial Light & Magic (ILM) to build the first linear CCD scanner for motion picture film scanning.

Kennel was also the architect of the Cineon digital film system in 1990 and led the development of the Cineon CCD film scanner and film recorder over the next couple of years. He helped launch Kodak's Cinesite Digital Film Center in 1992 and evangelized digital technology with the visual effects industry. He also provided technical support to Cinesite during the digital restoration of Disney's Snow White.

In 1993, Glenn Kennel was recognized by SMPTE with the Agfa-Gaevert Gold Medal for outstanding achievement in the field of film/television interface.

In 1995, he received the Academy Scientific and Technical Achievement award for the linear CCD film scanner, jointly developed with ILM. He worked with Philips to extend the Spirit Datacine to Cineon-compatible digital file output, first applying it to the film "Pleasantville" in 1997. He helped establish Cinesite's Digital Mastering department in 1998, providing technical support to the first major feature film to go through the DI process, "O Brother, Where Art Thou?" in 1999–2000.

As program manager of Kodak's Digital Cinema effort in 2000–2003, he led a team that developed servers and software for digital cinema and coordinated a joint development program with JVC for a digital cinema projector.

In 2003, Kennel left Kodak to work as an industry consultant with DCI on color encoding for digital cinema, including coordinating the digital mastering process for the ASC/DCI StEM test. He chaired the SMPTE DC28 ad hoc group on Color and helped draft several digital cinema standards. He joined Texas Instruments' DLP Cinema group in 2004, in a role that combined technology and business development for digital cinema, helping the industry address the practical hurdles to digital cinema deployment.

Kennel was elected to the Scientific and Technical Branch of the Academy of Motion Picture Arts and Sciences in 2005.

Kennel is now Vice President and General Manager of the Motion Picture division of Laser Pacific Media Corporation, where he is responsible for services including digital dailies, previews, Digital Intermediate, mastering and digital cinema packaging.

Kennel is the author of many technical papers on applications of digital technology to filmmaking published in the SMPTE *Journal*, and co-author of a chapter in *Understanding Digital Cinema* (2005). He is also a fellow of SMPTE.

About the Series Editor

Charles S. Swartz oversees efforts to further the entertainment industry through new technology. He draws from more than two decades of experience in feature film and television production, academic programming and strategic consulting to lead the center in identifying emerging entertainment technology issues and developing projects to study them. Swartz assumed his current position at the Entertainment Technology Center in 2003, where he has refocused and recharged the research center. He serves in two positions for SMPTE/Hollywood: Governor of the Hollywood Region and co-chair of the education committee. In 1996, the Los Angeles Business Journal named him one of 100 technology leaders in Los Angeles.

1
Overview of Color and Mastering for Digital Cinema

In June of 1999, George Lucas released his film "Star Wars: Episode 1" on two digital cinema screens—one in New York and one in Los Angeles. In the five years since this historic debut, over 150 films have been released digitally to over 500 screens in 30 countries around the world. These digital movies have played over 20,000 shows to satisfied audiences. Although digital cinema has not been widely promoted as a new and improved display method, educated audiences have shown a preference for digital over film presentation.

This book presents a survey of the development of color encoding and decoding standards for digital cinema distribution and exhibition. It describes the key issues and provides background on decisions that were made in the standardization process. Although the author was a key participant in the development of the SMPTE[1] DC28 documents, it is recommended that the reader refer to the published SMPTE standards[2] for the final word on implementation.

---

1. Society of Motion Picture and Television Engineers.
2. At the time of this writing, the SMPTE DC28 working group has several digital cinema documents in process. These standards are available to participants, but have not yet been published.

This book refers to colorimetric principles that are more rigorously defined in color textbooks[3,4] and assumes that the reader has a working knowledge of basic color principles and motion picture industry practices. However, one does not need to be a color scientist or industry insider to read and understand this book.

In late 1999, SMPTE established the DC28 working group to study the standardization requirements for digital cinema distribution, with the goal of establishing a world-wide standard. Since its standardization by SMPTE in 1916, the 35 mm motion picture film format has served as the single world-wide distribution standard for movies. 35 mm motion picture film has weathered the test of time, supporting major exhibition enhancements like sound, color, widescreen presentation and multi-track digital soundtracks, all compatible with 35 mm projection equipment based on the original standard. In today's hyper-competitive and fast-changing digital world, it seemed a tall order to establish a digital cinema distribution standard that would serve the industry for the next century. But the industry set its sights on just that. The goal was to develop a universal standard for digital cinema distribution that could be implemented in a cost effective way today, while also extensible to support future exhibition improvements.

The SMPTE DC28 group concluded its study work at the end of 2000 by identifying the need for standards for digital cinema mastering, distribution and exhibition. Working groups were established to address each of these areas. In addition, ad hoc groups of industry experts were formed to address specific issues, including packaging, key management and security, and color. The DC28 color ad hoc group began its work in 2002, focusing its initial discussions on the color encoding for digital cinema. The group was composed of experts from diverse parts of the industry that included studios, post production facilities and equipment manufacturers. While everyone agreed on the goal, there were many opinions on how best to get there.

While the SMPTE DC28 work proceeded slowly and steadily as a due process forum with diverse interests, the establishment in 2002 of the Digital Cinema Initiatives, LLC (DCI), a consortium formed by seven major Hollywood studios, provided a focus for the development of the digital cinema standards. A group of technical experts from the member studios met regularly to hammer out a consensus technical specification for digital cinema distribution. In its work, DCI used available and prototypical digital cinema equipment to evaluate requirements for compression, security, content packaging and color encoding. DCI hired several industry experts to supplement its internal expertise. Amongst other things, DCI funded the Contrast Sensitivity Test that verified the bit depth requirement for color encoding (see Chapter 4).

Most importantly, DCI provided a venue for the political process of building consensus amongst its members. Its crowning achievement was the delivery of a consensus technical specification for

---

3. R.W.B. Hunt, *The Reproduction of Color*, 6th Edition, Wiley, © 2004.
4. G. Wyszecki and W.S. Stiles, *Color Science: Concepts and Methods, Quantitative Data and Formulae*, 2nd Edition, Wiley, © 2000.

a 2 K/4 K scalable solution in July 2005 that was supported in its entirety by all of its members. This consensus specification removed a substantial uncertainty, paving the way for commercial deployment of compliant systems while substantially reducing the risk of technological obsolescence.

STUDIO OBJECTIVES

CTO Brad Hunt of the Motion Picture Association of America (MPAA) framed the work of DCI with the following ten goals:

1. **ENHANCED THEATRICAL EXPERIENCE**—The introduction of digital cinema must be used by the motion picture industry as an opportunity to significantly enhance the theatrical film experience and thus bring real benefits to theater audiences.

2. **QUALITY**—The picture and sound quality of digital cinema should present as accurately as possible the creative intent of the filmmaker. To that end, its quality must exceed the quality of a projected 35 mm "answer print" shown under optimum studio screening theater conditions. Any image compression that is used should be visually lossless.

3. **WORLDWIDE COMPATIBILITY**—The system should be based around global standards so that content can be distributed and played anywhere in the world as can be done today with a 35 mm film print.

4. **OPEN STANDARDS**—The components and technologies used should be based on open standards that foster competition amongst multiple vendors of equipment and services.

5. **INTEROPERABLE**—Each of the components of the system should be built around clearly defined standards and interfaces that insure interoperability between different equipment.

6. **EXTENSIBLE**—The hardware used in the system should be easily upgraded as advances in technology are made. This is especially important in evolving to higher quality levels.

7. **SINGLE INVENTORY**—Once a consensus on digital cinema standards is reached and implemented, upgrades to the system should be designed so that a single inventory of content can be distributed and compatibly played on all equipment installations.

8. **TRANSPORT**—The system should accommodate a variety of secure content transport mechanisms, including electronic as well as a physical media delivery.

9. **SECURE CONTENT PROTECTION**—The system must include a highly secure, end-to-end, conditional access content protection system, including digital rights management and content watermarking, because of the serious harm associated with the theft of digital content at this stage of its distribution life cycle. Playback devices must use on-line authentication with the decrypted content files never accessible in the clear.

10. **REASONABLE COST**—The system standards and mastering format(s) should be chosen so that the capital equipment and operational costs are reasonable. All required technology licenses should be available on reasonable and non-discriminatory terms.

The objectives that must be considered in the selection of color encoding standards for digital cinema distribution are an enhanced theatrical experience, with picture quality better than a film answer print[5], and open standards that are interoperable and extensible. And all of this must be supported by equipment and operational costs that are reasonable. In addition, since the transition to digital distribution cannot happen overnight and will likely take 5 to 10 years, it is important that the mastering process and the end product be compatible with traditional 35 mm film distribution and exhibition practices.

This compatibility with 35 mm film locked down two major exhibition requirements: screen luminance and chromaticity. Creative color decisions that affect the look and feel of the picture are part of the mastering process. For the creative intent to be faithfully reproduced on the cinema screen, it is critical that the screen luminance and white point be standardized. And since movies will be exhibited on both film and digital projectors for some time, it is critical that these parameters be consistent in both venues. For compatibility with legacy film projectors, the digital cinema standards specify a screen luminance of 48 cd/m^2 (14 ft L) with a white point of 0.314 x, 0.351 y. The basis for these parameters will be explained in Chapter 5.

This treatment of digital cinema color encoding will describe the standards and practices that are used to create the digital cinema master, and those that are used to faithfully reproduce this master in cinema exhibition. Since this process does not include color calibration or color encoding for image origination, front-end production is excluded from this analysis. Instead, the book focuses on the middle to the end of the process, as shown by the highlighted blocks in Figure 1.1, and the color calibration and standards that support mastering and distribution. Origination, dailies,

---

5. An answer print is the first print that combines picture and sound and is a first generation graded print from the original negative.

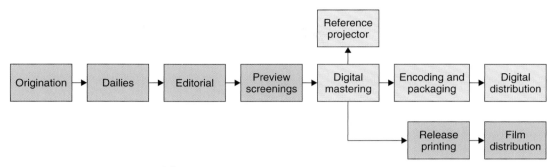

Figure 1-1. Motion Picture Workflow.

editing and preview functions are outside of the scope of this book. Color encoding for digital cinema distribution picks up in the digital mastering process (where the final color grading is performed on a calibrated reference projector). The complimentary process of color decoding is performed on a calibrated projector in the cinema.

Now, here's a quick preview of the rest of the book.

Chapter 2, "Color in Film", covers the color characteristics of the traditional motion picture film system, starting with the exposure of an image on a color negative film. The extended range of a typical negative film is described, along with typical placement of a white card and 18% gray for normal and over-exposures. The characteristics of color print film are then described, along with the "print-through" curves that result when a negative is printed onto print stock. The IP/IN release printing process is discussed.

Chapter 3, "Color Space", starts with a review of the basic characteristics of human vision, and how color scientists have developed experimental methods to model it. After reviewing the requirements for the selection of a color space for digital cinema, the various options are summarized. The experimental basis for the CIE colorimetric analysis is reviewed, leading to the standard x, y, z color matching functions and the X, Y and Z color primaries.

Chapter 4, "Transfer Function", covers the definition of the non-linear (gamma 1/2.6) encoding transfer function selected for digital cinema distribution. DCI conducted an experiment to verify that the Barten model for contrast sensitivity applies to theatrical viewing conditions, and the results of this test are described.

Chapter 5, "Reference Projector and Environment", covers the definition of a reference projector for digital cinema mastering and exhibition, for the purpose of insuring consistency from screen to screen. The important image attributes are defined along with appropriate tolerances for mastering and exhibition. The calibration and measurement of digital cinema projectors is reviewed, with a brief description of the instrumentation and test patterns required.

Chapter 6, "Digital Mastering", reviews the evolving trends in mastering, including the widespread adoption of a digital intermediate process that supports the digital conforming and grading of the full feature film, while supporting outputs to everything from film release prints, to digital cinema distribution masters (DCDMs) and home video masters. The workflow of the digital intermediate process is reviewed, along with the choices of working resolution (2 K or 4 K) and color calibration (film-centric or digital-centric).

Chapter 7, "Color Encoding for Digital Cinema Distribution", describes the color transforms in converting from the RGB mastering space to XYZ color encoding. The rationale for the output-referred color encoding is reviewed. The draft SMPTE standards also include the definition of metadata from the reference projector to facilitate gamut mapping downstream.

Chapter 8, "Projector Color Processing", covers the processing requirements for a digital cinema projector. Calibration is critical to provide consistency from screen to screen and over time. When wider gamut projectors are introduced in the future, a gamut mapping capability will need to be implemented in legacy projectors in order to maintain backward compatibility. Finally, the advantages of relative luminance encoding are reviewed in the context of a practical test.

Chapter 9, "DLP Cinema — A Case Study" describes how the leading digital cinema projection technology from Texas Instruments works, and its historical development in response to industry needs. This includes an explanation of the color processing and calibration technology built into DLP Cinema projectors.

Chapter 10, "Digital Display Technologies", provides a brief overview of other display technologies used in the professional and consumer markets. These include D-ILA™ and SXRD™ for digital projection, and LCD, plasma, and SED flat panel displays. The ubiquitous CRT reference monitor in post production seems to be at the end of its run, but it is not clear which digital display technology will replace it. The limitations of today's displays are reviewed, along with some new techniques that promise to overcome the shortcomings.

Chapter 11, "Digital 3D Presentation", describes the history and fundamental technology behind theatrical 3D presentation. The light efficiency of various options is compared, including dual projectors with linear polarizers, single projector with shuttered glasses, single projector with Z-screen™ active polarizer, and dual projectors with Infitec™ color bandpass filters.

Chapter 12, "The Future", reviews the driving forces behind the deployment of digital cinema systems and takes a stab at predicting how fast this may occur. The importance of alternative content is reviewed along with the additional technical requirements. Digital cameras are just being introduced that are beginning to challenge the dynamic range and color gamut of traditional motion picture negative films, but the device-independent XYZ color encoding for digital cinema distribution can easily accommodate new image sources. Color appearance modeling techniques promise to help automate the process of color conversion for different displays. Finally, the book concludes with a brief discussion of the archival dilemma with digital storage technologies and some recommendations on which elements to archive.

2
Color in Motion Picture Film

Before diving into the details of color in digital cinema, let's step back and review how color is captured, creatively manipulated and displayed in the traditional motion picture film system. This chapter covers the basic design and performance of the negative/positive motion picture film system, and the characteristics that control the color gamut and contrast of the reproduced picture. It also examines the fundamental differences between film and video, and how this affects their respective production processes.

A color negative film is used for original photography, and its basic function is to capture the scene. For motion pictures, this film is printed onto a color positive print film that is used for projection display. The basic characteristics of the color negative film and the color print film and the placement of image information on these films control the color and contrast of the resulting picture.

Color Negative Film

The characteristic curves for a typical motion picture color negative film are shown in Figure 2.1. The three curves represent the red, green and blue color records, which are reproduced by cyan, magenta, and yellow dyes, respectively. The three curves are offset vertically because the base density of the negative film is orange in color (it contains more yellow and magenta dye than cyan dye).

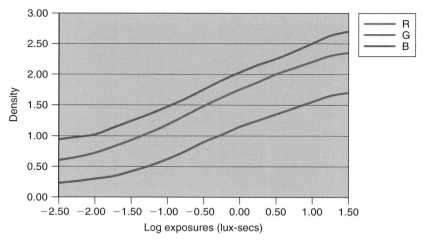

Figure 2-1.   Kodak 5218 Color Negative Film.

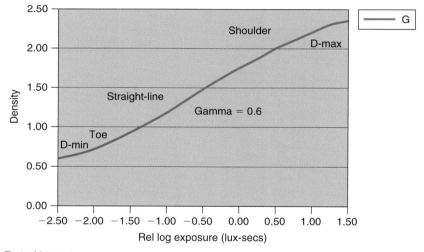

Figure 2-2.   Typical Negative.

Film characteristic curves are produced by plotting density versus relative log exposure. Density is defined as the negative logarithm of film transmittance, so this is a log/log plot. The higher the density, the more light is blocked in that channel. In this figure, the 90% white card is used as the reference point for normal exposure, corresponding to zero relative log exposure on the x-axis.

In order to simplify the following illustrations, the typical negative film will be represented by the single curve shown in Figure 2.2. The placement of image information and subsequent transformations apply to all three records in the color film. The color offset between the three records is removed in the process of printing the color negative film to reproduce neutral grays on the color print.

The characteristic curve of a typical negative film has five regions: D-min (minimum density), the toe, the straight-line portion, the shoulder, and D-max (maximum density). Exposures of less than 1% of the reference white card (just under seven stops of camera exposure) or −2.0 relative log exposure will be recorded as Dmin. The toe is the portion of the curve where the slope increases gradually with increasing exposure.

The straight-line is the portion of the characteristic curve with constant slope. For optimum scene capture and subsequent reproduction, the camera exposure should be adjusted to place all significant image information within the straight-line portion. The slope of the straight-line portion is known as the gamma of the film. The gamma of a typical motion picture color negative film is 0.6.

The shoulder is the portion of the curve where the slope decreases with increasing exposure. Film introduces a "soft clip", with exposures in excess of ten times above the white card (three stops) or 1.0 relative log exposure recorded as Dmax.

The nominal placement of a 90% white card, 18% gray card, and 2% black card for a normal camera exposure are shown in Figure 2.3. The 18% gray card is a commonly used test object in film photography. A 90% white card is typically used to set the white level of television cameras. The 2% black is shown for additional reference. Flatly-lit interior scenes often have a contrast range of 50:1 or less. Exterior scenes with shadows may have a contrast range of 100:1 or even greater.

CONTRAST

The term contrast has many meanings. In original photography, contrast range refers to the ratio of the peak white to the darkest black in the scene. In a projected print, contrast refers to the slope of the transfer function, which in film is also known as gamma. In addition, display systems are often characterized by two very different contrast measurements. Sequential contrast refers to the ratio of measured luminances between a maximum (white) and minimum (black) applied signal. Intra-frame contrast measures the localized contrast within a frame and is measured with a checkerboard pattern.

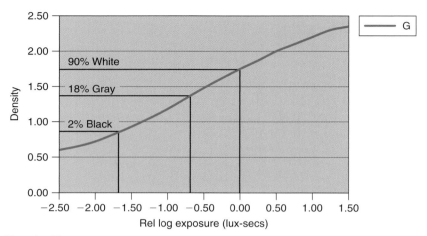

Figure 2-3. Negative Placement.

The latitude of the film is defined as the total range of exposure that results in a recorded density change. The latitude of a typical motion picture negative film is 3.0 log exposure, or a scene contrast range of 1000 to 1. This corresponds to approximately 10 camera stops (each stop represents a factor of 2 in exposure).

Several other important observations can be made from the characteristic curve for a typical negative film. The range above 90% white is the overexposure latitude of the film, and is about 1.0 log exposure (10:1 in exposure). This extra overhead accommodates specular highlights and bright lights in the original photography and provides a comfortable margin for overexposure. The shoulder of the negative film induces a gentle highlight compression that is more natural than the hard clip implemented in video cameras. Likewise, the toe of the negative film also induces a gentle shadow compression.

Color Print Film

The characteristic curves for a typical motion picture color print film are shown in Figure 2.4. The gamma and density range of the color print is higher than that of the color negative film. The curve is "S"-shaped with only a short straight-line portion. The midscale gamma of a typical color print film is about 2.8.

When a color negative film is printed onto color print film, the resulting print-through curve is shown in Figure 2.5. In the ideal case, the color is balanced so that all three curves overlay throughout the full scale. The normal placement of the 90% white card, 18% gray card, and 2% black card on color print film is also shown in Figure 2.5. Note that the horizontal axis represents the relative

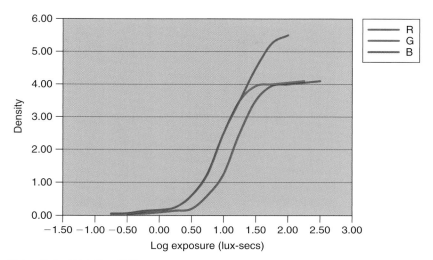

Figure 2-4. Vision Color Print Film 5383.

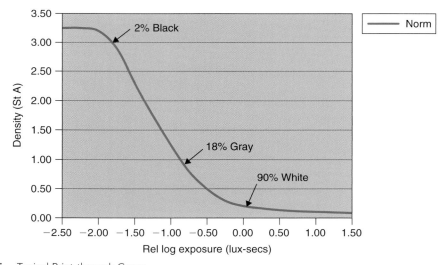

Figure 2-5. Typical Print-through Curve.

log exposure of the camera negative film that was printed onto the print film. The resulting gamma of the print element has a maximum mid-scale value of 1.7, which gets reduced by typical projection flare to about 1.5. This 50% gamma boost when compared to the original scene produces a visually pleasing grayscale when the print film is projected in a darkened surround.[1]

---

1. R.W.B. Hunt, *The Reproduction of Color*, 6th Edition, Wiley, © 2004, p.55.

In addition to the highlight compression induced by the shoulder of the negative film, the toe of the print film also induces further highlight compression.

Printing Heavy Negatives

It is common practice to over-expose negative films, when light levels permit, to reduce graininess, saturate colors, or for other creative reasons.

When a negative film is overexposed, the result is a "heavy" negative, or one in which the densities are heavier (higher) than those on a normally exposed negative film. The placement of the 90% white, 18% gray, and 2% black cards all shift up the scale, as illustrated in Figure 2.6, for an over-exposure of two stops. If a print were made using the standard printer exposure settings, the resulting print-through curve would look like Figure 2.7. The whites would appear compressed, blacks would be washed out, and the overall scene would appear flat and lacking in contrast.

The heavy negative film can be "printed down" by increasing the printer exposure to compensate. When this is done, the resulting print-through curve (Figure 2.8) looks much like that of the normally exposed negative film, except that the shoulder of the curve is extended. Over-exposing the negative and then printing it down can extend the blacks, darkening deep shadows if the scene has a wide contrast range.

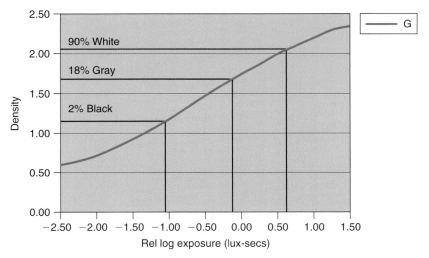

Figure 2-6. 2 Stops Over-Exposure.

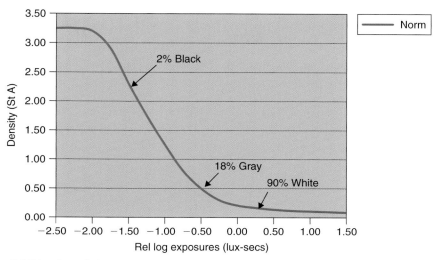

Figure 2-7.   2-0 Print-through Curve.

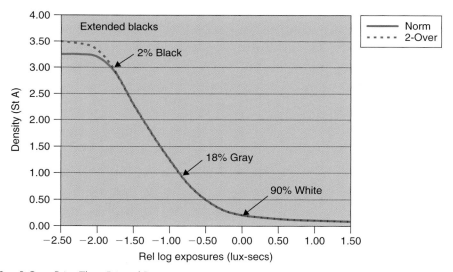

Figure 2-8.   2-Over Print-Thru, Printed Down.

Selective Color Timing

The traditional term for the control of color in motion picture printing is color timing, or (outside of the US) color grading. Color is controlled in terms of printer "lights", sometimes called printer "points". Each printer light corresponds to an exposure change of 0.025 log exposure, or 1/12th of a stop. With a typical range of 50 printer lights, this provides plus or minus 2 stops of printer exposure from the mid-range setting of 25.

Most motion picture printers have an additive light source. The illumination (generally Xenon) is split into red, green and blue beams using dichroic color separation filters. Each of these beams is modulated by mechanical light valves (think of Venetian blinds) that are capable of changing within milliseconds to make color changes from scene to scene. Typical printers used for color timing run at a frame rate of no more than 180 feet per minute, so this can be done between frames without any visible gradient.[2]

The process of color timing is more than simply adjusting for the exposure of the original negative or the color temperature of the lighting that was used in original photography. If this were all that was necessary, these adjustments could be automated with a sampling of the average densities of the color records on the negative film. In fact, this automated practice is typically used by photofinishers to generate consumer prints.

But color timing is also a creative process, where creative choices are made by skilled timers, working closely with cinematographers. Because the print film can only reproduce a fraction of the contrast range of the original negative (approximately 400:1 rather than 1000:1 in terms of scene exposure), a key part of the printing process is selecting that part of the contrast range that is most important to telling the story. Furthermore, a scene may be printed down (made darker) to create a dark, somber mood or to intentionally hide details in the shadows.

Color balance is also used creatively to communicate emotion or provide context in a story. A vivid example of this is the dramatic color changes used by Director Steven Soderbergh in the film "Out of Sight", where the hot, humid Florida scenes were colored a strong yellow and the gritty, cold streets of Detroit were colored a deep blue.

So, the cinematographer's craft includes the lighting and exposure of the original negative (the capture function), as well as directions on how to print the negative (the color timing or grading function) to reproduce the important details in the shot and to communicate the intended emotion. In the motion picture film system, these two functions are separated.

There are several reasons why this separation between capture and color grading offers advantages. First, no time is wasted on color grading on the set, while the talent and supporting technicians are standing by waiting for the next shot. Secondly, it enhances the cinematographer's creative control of the picture.

---

2. Dominic Case, *Film Technology in Post Production*, Focal Press, © Dominic Case 1997.

For example, if shadow details in a high contrast scene are important, the cinematographer can overexpose the shot, knowing that he can print it down in post production, preserving the overall brightness and contrast, while extending the range into the shadows, uncovering details that might otherwise have been lost.

Conversely, if highlight details are most important, say in a fire or explosion, the cinematographer may choose to underexpose the shot, so that he is assured of capturing the full range of highlight information.

THE TRADITIONAL VIDEO PROCESS

Unlike film, the traditional video process is much simpler, but these simplifications result in creative restrictions. Typically, the camera is white-balanced on the set and a 90% white card is used to set the peak white at 100% video level. A technician monitors the video signal levels to make sure that they don't exceed 110% (where they will be clipped) or fall too low. The director can look at the picture on a monitor to judge not only composition, but also color. If he has a calibrated monitor in a trailer or tent with controlled lighting, then he has a true WYSIWYG (what you see is what you get) situation.

For studio production of live television shows, a practice of "shading" the cameras with test targets led to "painting" the cameras subjectively with a camera control unit to get the desired look on screen. To some degree, this practice has been adopted by directors and cameramen shooting episodic television. Many modern video cameras offer a range of controls for custom calibration, including custom gamma tables with "knees" for highlight compression and custom color matrices.

Although video is edited and conformed in post production, artistic color correction is generally much more limited than with film. First of all, color correction is not required for exposure control or scene to scene color balance, because these things are taken care of at the set. But equally important, the range of creative control is severely restricted by the calibration of the camera on the set and by the limited dynamic range of the video signal that was recorded. Unlike film, which has an over-exposure latitude of approximately three stops, a typical video recording has very limited headroom.

Spectral Sensitivity of Color Negative Film

The spectral sensitivities of the three records of a color negative film define the color gamut (range of colors) that can be captured by that film. Figure 2.9 shows the spectral sensitivity curves

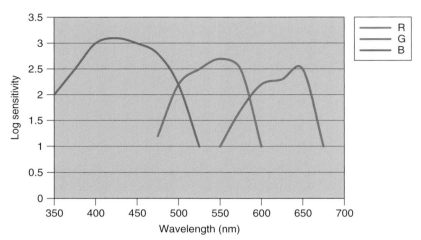

Figure 2-9.   Log Spectral Sensitivity 5218.

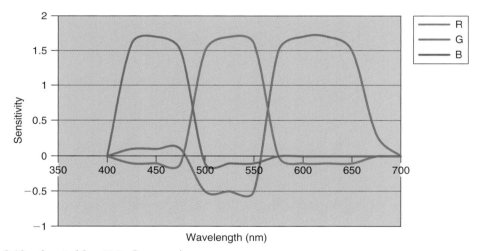

Figure 2-10.   Spectral Sensitivity Compared.

of a typical color negative motion picture film, plotted as log sensitivity versus wavelength, with an individual curve for each of the red, green and blue sensitive layers of the film. Sensitivity is defined as the reciprocal of the exposure (in ergs/cm^2) required to produce a specified density, generally a density of 1.0 above D-min.

The color matching functions for a typical television camera, after matrixing to ITU Rec. 709 primaries, is shown in Figure 2.10.

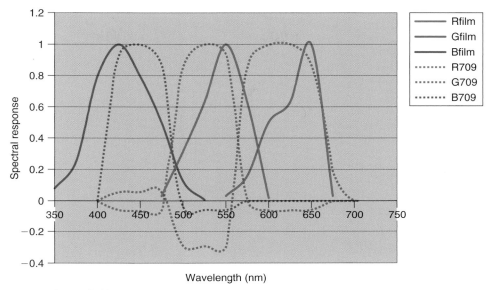

Figure 2-10a. CMFs of 709 Camera.

The film spectral sensitivities can be linearized and normalized for comparison to the color matching functions of the ITU Rec. 709 camera, as shown in Figure 2.10a. The individual color records of the film show narrower peaks with a shorter blue peak and longer red peak, leading to a larger separation between the records.

Image Dyes of Color Negative Film

The red, green and blue color records of the negative film are recorded by image dyes, once the latent image has been developed by chemical processing. These image dyes have important spectral characteristics that control how the captured colors are reproduced on the print film. The spectral dye density curves of a typical color negative motion picture film are shown in Figure 2.11, plotted as diffuse spectral density versus wavelength.

An ideal color dye would absorb light only in its own region of the spectrum. But real color dyes absorb some light at other wavelengths. This is called unwanted absorption, and if uncorrected, would cause color desaturation and hue shifts. Color negative films, however, are designed with built-in chemical color correction in the form of colored couplers. These colored couplers create an orange mask in the film D-min. Since these colored couplers are developed to form image dyes, they provide a compensating masking to correct for the effects of unwanted dye absorption when the negative is printed.

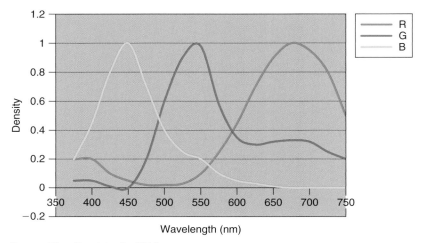

Figure 2-11.   Spectral Dye Densities for 5218.

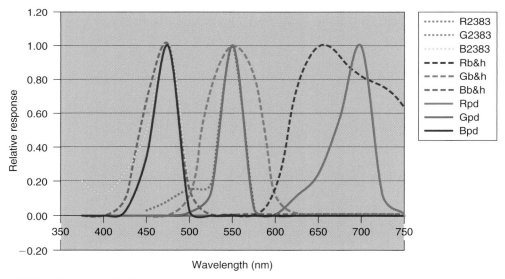

Figure 2-12.   Printing Density Spec Response.

Printing Density

Printing density is the term for how the densities of the color negative film are "seen" by the color print film. The response of the print film is the combination of the spectral sensitivities of the print stock and the spectral output of the light source used in the printer. This is generated by

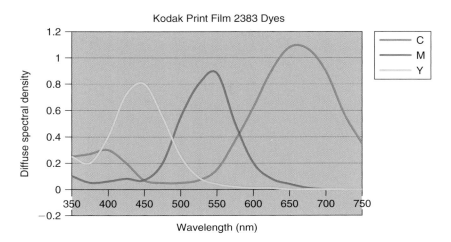

Figure 2-13.   Kodak Print Film 2383 Dyes.

convolving the spectral output of the printer with the spectral sensitivities of the print film, as shown in Figure 2.12.

Image Dyes of the Color Print Film

The color print film reproduces its color records with three image dyes. These image dyes, when combined with the spectral output of a typical projector, define the color gamut of a projected motion picture film print. Color image dyes for a typical motion picture print film are shown in Figure 2.13.

Notice that the film color gamut was not described in terms of "primaries", because the color record is actually created by subtractive dyes (cyan, magenta and yellow in color) that take away light, rather than add light to the image. So the most saturated red (primary) color is created by a minimum of cyan dye and a maximum of magenta and yellow. This is very different from a television display or a digital cinema projector, both of which create their pictures through an additive combination of red, green and blue primaries (see Chapter 5). In an additive video display, the most saturated red is created by turning on the red primary and turning off the green and blue. Figure 2.14 compares the linearized spectral transmission of the red, green and blue records of Kodak 2383 print film to the spectral output of a DLP Cinema® projector[3]. To make this comparison, the film dye densities were linearized and converted to transmission, with the complementary channels multiplied to construct red, green and blue transmission for comparison.

---

3. Pinot, Christie Digital Systems, 2003.

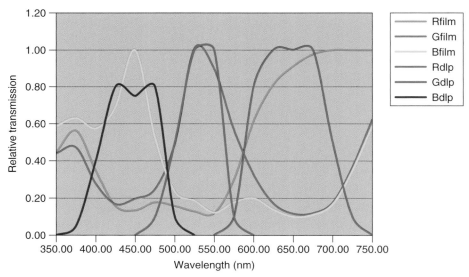

Figure 2-14. Film and DLP Cinema.

Unstable Primaries

Due to complexities in the underlying chemical formulations that are beyond the scope of this summary, the film printing system contains lots of cross-talk between the individual color records, resulting in a condition sometimes referred to as "unstable primaries". The result is that a range of colors is reproduced not as a straight vector, but as a curve. This is very different from the behavior of an additive digital display where the three color channels are independent. Figure 2.15 compares a series of color wedges on film and digital.

Furthermore, it means that the most saturated colors that film can reproduce are dark cyans, magentas and yellows, each produced by a maximum density of its respective image dye, but resulting in low luminance levels. In contrast, the most saturated colors on a digital display are the bright red, green and blue primaries, each produced by the maximum output of its additive color channel, and therefore resulting in the maximum luminance for that channel.

Film Color Gamut

The characterization of the color gamut of color print film is more complicated than simply bounding a set of color primaries, as one would do in an additive digital display. The best way to

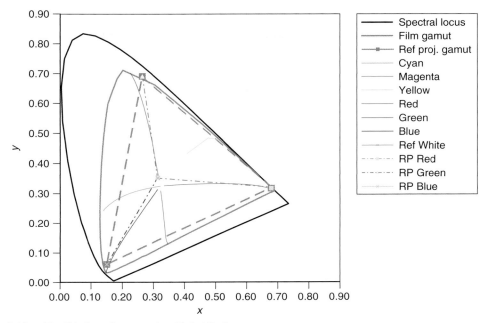

Figure 2-15. Film Wedges Compared to Digital Projector.

do this is to generate a series of color exposure wedges and to measure the resulting chromaticity coordinates when these patches are projected. The color gamut of motion picture print film is shown in Figure 2.16 in a typical x, y chromaticity plot. It should be noted that the gamut is actually a three dimensional solid, with the third dimension being luminance. In three dimensions this solid is shaped somewhat like a potato.

The importance of this will become clear as we discuss the steps necessary to match a color print with a digital display. Also note that the film print can reproduce a wider color gamut than a digital projector, particularly in the cyan to green region.

Film Contrast

The print-through curve for a negative printed to Kodak Vision 2383 film print was shown in Figure 2.5. While the in-frame contrast is further reduced by flare, the sequential (or peak contrast of the system) is derived by subtracting the D-min from the D-max and raising this density difference to the power of 10. In this case, the density range of 3.2 corresponds to a contrast ratio of about 1600:1, which compares closely to the capabilities of today's digital cinema projectors.

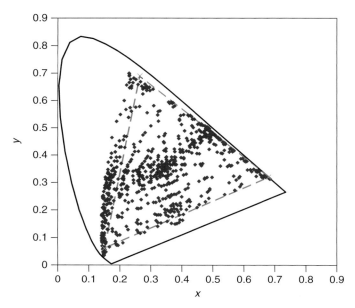

Figure 2-16.   Measured Film Data Compared to Reference Projector.

In 1997, Kodak introduced a higher contrast print film, Vision Premier, which has seen limited use. This premium print stock boosts the contrast of the overall picture and provides deeper blacks. Figure 2.17 compares the projected print-through curves of Vision and Vision Premier print films. The density range of approximately 3.6 for Vision Premier corresponds to a contrast ratio of nearly 4,000:1, which exceeds the capabilities of today's digital cinema projectors.

It is important to note that this represents the maximum sequential contrast ratio that can be reproduced by a typical print film, from the brightest white (D-min) to the darkest black (D-max) and that these conditions are never achieved within a single frame. A very high contrast picture may exhibit an intra-frame contrast of only 200:1. So the deeper blacks are most readily seen (and have the greatest impact) as the picture fades to black.

Dailies, Answer Prints and Release Prints

During the production process, film negatives are processed each night and printed for review the next morning, a process called "Dailies" or "Rushes". In this process, the color timer is not trying to craft the final color of the picture, but rather to produce a quick print that can be used by the cinematographer and director to judge composition, lighting and action, as well as technical details like focus and overall exposure. Importantly, the cinematographer receives feedback on

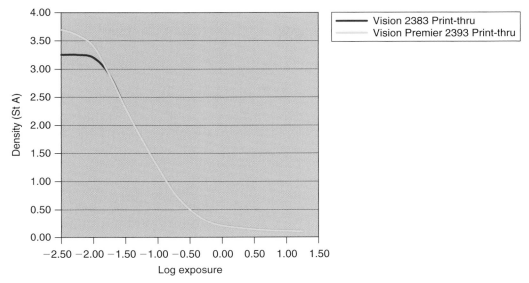

Figure 2-17.   Comparison of Print-thru Curves.

the exposure of each scene by reading the printer lights that were selected by the color timer. With the digitization of this process, and the increasing use of digital dailies, this important feedback mechanism can be lost.

In the traditional process, the film negative is conformed to an Edit Decision List (EDL). Generally called "Neg Cutting", this process involves the careful pulling of select shots using the film keycode (footage and frame counts burned into the raw stock) and the splicing of these shots to build a composite reel for printing.

This is where the color timer really shows his skill. Working under the direction of the cinematographer as to how each scene should look, he creates a trial print for review with the cinematographer. Several steps are needed before the print is ready to review. First, there is the laborious process of rolling, rewinding and re-rolling the film projector to study each shot and make notes of the printer light changes required. Recent advances in film projection equipment, such as the Kinoton electronic transport and Technicolor's Realtime Color Timing process have improved the efficiency of this task.

The color timer's notes are then translated into timing lights and these lights are typed in sequence to create the paper tape (timing metadata) that is used to drive the printer. A printer operator loads the printer with the original negative, the timing tape and a roll of print raw stock and produces a print. Loading the raw stock and making the print is done in the dark, with the assistance of a very dim, yellow safelight.

The print raw stock must be processed by other technicians, along with the other rolls going through the lab. The combination of these sequential steps, and the coordination of the many people involved in the production process, means that the typical turnaround time for each color timing pass is next day.

Typically, the team of color timer and cinematographer will work on one reel (up to 2000 feet in length or approx. 20 minutes of running time) of a movie at a time, finishing that reel before they move on to the next. When the full movie is finished and approved, this final print is called an "Answer Print". This answer print is the highest quality print that will ever be screened as it is struck directly from the original negative.

Film prints are duplicated for distribution by creating intermediate elements, using color intermediate stock, that are used for high speed release printing. The first step is to make an Inter-Positive or "timed IP", so called because the timing lights from the answer print are used to make a color-corrected positive intermediate. This IP is then printed again to produce an Inter-Negative (IN) or duplicate negative element. This two-step duplicating process works because the intermediate film has a gamma of 1.0, so it maintains the original contrast.

The IN functions as a timed duplicate of the original negative, but multiple copies can be made to support the production of several thousand release prints (a "wide" release can have as many as 3-5,000 prints or more). Typically, an individual IN produced on durable polyester base can be used for striking 1,000 prints, or with careful handling, as many as 2,000 prints. These release prints are generated on high speed release printers that run at speeds of 2,000 feet per minute or higher. Since the standard projection rate of 24 frames per second equates to 90 feet per minute, this means that these release printers run more than 20 times faster than the real-time playback rate. This duplication efficiency is unmatched in the digital world.

A carefully produced release print, with the tightest laboratory control of the color negative and print film chemical development processes, produces a print that visually matches the color and contrast of the answer print. In practice, it is typical to see a slight pickup in contrast and small color shifts in the release print, along with subtle to substantial variations from print to print due to process variations in the chemical print film development process. The major film laboratories run high-speed, high temperature print processes for release printing to improve efficiency. Unfortunately, this also means that the "gain" is turned up and variations tend to be amplified, meaning that substantial drift often occurs from day to day.

Since reels are typically finalized sequentially, and the release printing process for each reel starts when the answer print for that reel is approved, there can be substantial color changes due to the print process variations from reel to reel. Typically, the editor makes reel changes on scene changes to minimize the detection of these color shifts. However, it is not uncommon to see a major color shift at the reel change.

Furthermore, since film duplication is an analog, optical printing process that involves an additional two film generations, the release print inevitably loses a little sharpness. It also picks up a little extra graininess and unsteadiness in the duplication process. These losses can be minimized with good quality control, but they cannot be eliminated. Digital cinema distribution eliminates both the losses and the color shifts inherent in analog film distribution.

Cineon Digital Film System

In the design of the Cineon Digital Film System, Kodak engineers set out to provide a digital intermediate representation that was compatible and complementary to the traditional film system, allowing the output of the digital film process to be inter-cut seamlessly with live action footage for conventional printing.

The Digital Negative produced by the Cineon Digital Film Scanner is a digital representation of the typical negative film. This has several important characteristics.

Full Latitude

The Cineon scanner is calibrated for a 2.048 density range: this allows it to capture the full latitude (density range) of the negative film with some margin at top and bottom. The scanner light source is balanced on film D-min, so that the resulting digital image will have a neutral color balance if the film was exposed at the correct color temperature. The Digital Negative includes significant headroom above the nominal white point to handle over-exposed negative films and scenes with a wide contrast range.

10 bits

With 10 bits per color over a 2.048 density range, the resulting quantization step size is 0.002 D per code value. This exceeds the threshold for contour visibility, which insures that no contour artifacts (also known as banding) will be visible in images.

At the time of the original development in 1990, there was much debate over the extra burden of storing and processing 10 bits per color channel rather than the 8 bits widely used in digital video systems of that era. But these extra two bits also allowed the Cineon scanner to capture the extended headroom of the negative film, and preserve the creative flexibility to digitally

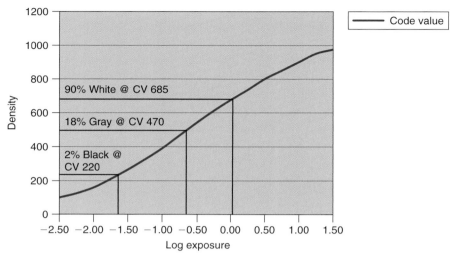

Figure 2-18.   Cineon Digital Negative.

"print" the processed scenes up or down in post production without introducing clipping arti-facts. Likewise the digital duplicate negative produced at the output of the process contains the full range, so it can also be printed up or down without creative compromise.

Printing Density

The Cineon Digital Negative is represented in printing density, which is to say, the density that is "seen" by the print film when the negative is printed with a standard illuminant. The illumination and color filters in the Cineon scanner were designed so that the effective spectral response of the scanner matches that of print film.

Normal Digital Negative

The characteristic curve for the Cineon Digital Negative is shown in Figure 2.18. For a normally exposed negative film, the 90% white card has a code value of 685, the 18% gray card has a code value of 470, and the 2% black card has a code value of 220. These target code values assume that the scanner was calibrated to a code value of 95 for D-min.

Heavy Digital Negative

For a heavy negative, the code values of the 90% white, 18% gray, and 2% black cards are shifted higher. The Digital Negative resulting from a heavy negative that was over-exposed by 2 stops is

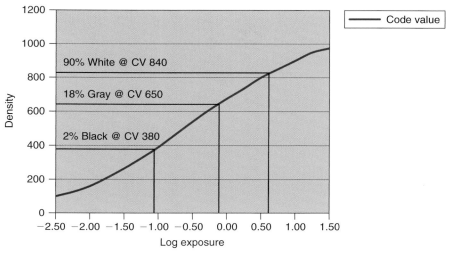

Figure 2-19.   Cineon Digital Negative (2 stops over-exposed).

shown in Figure 2.19. This results in 90% white at 840 code value, 18% gray at 650 code value, and 2% black at 380 code value. In order to compensate for the overexposure, the Digital Negative can be "printed down" by subtracting a code value offset of 180. With a typical negative film gamma of 0.6, each stop in exposure offsets the Digital Negative by 90 code values (in the midscale).

Digital Duplicate Negative

To make a film recording of the Digital Negative, it is necessary to understand the characteristics of the output film stock and the laser film recorder and to calibrate the system accordingly.

Cineon Laser Film Recorder

The Cineon Laser Film Recorder produces a film duplicate negative from the Digital Negative data that matches the color and density range of the original negative. This duplicate negative is produced on fine-grain Eastman Color Intermediate Film EXR 5244 (later replaced by 2244). The duplicate negative is exposed so that a code value of 445 is mapped to a Status M density of 1.00 R, 1.50 G, and 1.60 B, consistent with the Laboratory Aim Density (LAD) process widely used for printer control.

Kodak recommends that a LAD patch be recorded on the head end of each job and that this LAD patch be used to control subsequent printing stages. When a print is made from the duplicate negative film, the LAD patch is printed to Status A densities of 1.09 R, 1.06 G, and 1.03 B.

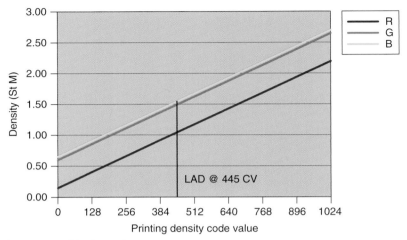

Figure 2-20.   Cineon Laser Film Recorder.

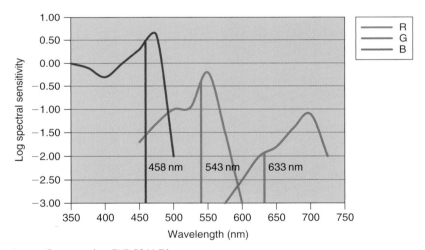

Figure 2-21.   Lasers Compared to EXR 5244 Film.

A typical calibration curve for the digital duplicate negative produced by the Cineon Laser Film Recorder is shown in Figure 2.20[4]. The 10 bits of printing density (1024 code values) cover a range of 2.048 density.

The lasers used in the Cineon Laser Film Recorder were selected to match the peak spectral sensitivities of Eastman Color Intermediate Film EXR 5244, as shown in Figure 2.21[5]. The full density

---

4. G. Kennel, "Digital Film Scanning and Recording: The Technology and Practice", SMPTE Journal, March 1994, p.180.
5. Ibid, p.179.

range can be exposed with minimum cross-color exposure, so a full range of colors are reproduced with accurate hue and saturation.

Although Kodak discontinued its Cineon Digital Film System in 1998, the Cineon file format, digital film scanners and laser film recorders are still used in the industry. The 10-bit log printing-density and calibration methodologies have been picked up and implemented by other manufacturers of digital film scanning and laser recording equipment, most notably Imagica, Filmlight, Thomson and Arri.

3
Color Space for Digital Cinema

Historically, color imaging systems have used a variety of tri-chromatic color encoding approaches, commonly called color spaces. Representing color as additive mixtures of three stimuli is based on research and characterization of the human visual system, and can be traced to properties of the underlying photo-sensitive receptors on the retina of the human eye.

The photo-receptors in the eye fall into two categories, rods and cones, so called for their physical shape. Color vision is derived from the output of the cones at normal levels of illumination. This photopic vision requires luminances of several cd/m^2 or more. There are three types of cones, sensitive to long, medium, and short regions of the human visual spectrum, nominally referred to as red, green and blue types. These three types of cones are distributed randomly on the retina, but there are many fewer blue cones than red or green ones.

At very low levels of light (below a few hundredths of a cd/m^2), human vision relies on the rods which are monochromatic. This is called scotopic vision. Cinema presentation covers the range from peak white at 48 cd/m^2 to blacks as low as 0.02 cd/m^2, so it approaches scotopic light levels. Mesopic vision is the term for the visual response at intermediate light levels where this response comes from a mixture of rods and cones. The blacks in a cinema presentation clearly fall in the mesopic region. Figure 3.1 shows the spectral sensitivity of the eye, comparing

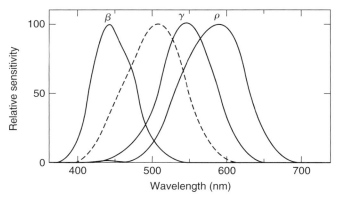

Figure 3-1. Spectral Sensitivity of the Human Eye (Source: R.W.G. Hunt, "Measuring Color", Third Edition, Fountain Press, England, © 1998, p.21.)

the photopic responses of the red, green and blue-sensitive cones to the scotopic response of the rods.

One of the important foundations of color science is Grassmann's empirical laws that describe the color-matching properties of additive mixtures of color stimuli (p. 322 Hunt):

1. Three independent variables are necessary and sufficient to specify a color match,

2. For an additive mixture of color stimuli, only their tristimulus values are relevant, not their spectral compositions,

3. In an additive mixture of color stimuli, if one or more components of the mixture are gradually changed, the resulting tristimulus values also change gradually.

The motion picture color negative film that was described in Chapter 2 captures the scene in three red, green and blue records, with these images recorded as subtractive cyan, magenta and yellow image dyes. When the color negative is printed, the negative dyes modulate the exposure in three red, green and blue records of the print film, creating a positive image constructed with complimentary cyan, magenta and yellow dyes. It should be noted that the first commercial color motion picture system was the Technicolor two-strip process that recorded color in two bands (red and green), but this system required extreme measures in art direction and wardrobe to control the colors on the set and could not faithfully reproduce natural colors without a blue channel.

Color television signals are generated from cameras which capture red, green and blue signals with individual tubes or CCD sensors from the original scene. These same red, green and blue signals are reproduced on a television display, with each signal modulating the amplitude of its respective red, green and blue phosphor on a cathode ray tube (CRT) display. However, in order to conserve bandwidth for storage and transmission, color television signals are transcoded to luminance (Y) and two chrominance channels (u and v). These channels are generated from the captured R, G and B channels by applying a linear matrix.

By transforming the signal into luminance and chrominance components, one is able to take advantage of an important characteristic of human vision—the eye is most sensitive to detail in luminance information. This means that the bandwidth of the two chrominance channels can be reduced without substantially impacting the quality of the color picture. In NTSC (so called for the National Television Standards Committee that established the color encoding for US television broadcast in 1953) the bandwidth of the broadcast luminance channel is 4.2 MHz, while the bandwidths of the u and v chrominance channels are 1.5 and 0.5 MHz, respectively.

The NTSC color transformation from red, green and blue to luminance and chrominance, and its reconstruction, if done reversibly, does not change the gamut or the quality of the signal. So the color space is defined by the gamut of the original red, green and blue signals. However, the bandwidth-limiting process does remove chrominance detail and the quadrature modulation of the two chrominance channels on a color sub-carrier, while an extremely clever way to make the broadcast color signal backward-compatible to pre-existing monochrome television sets, did result in decoding artifacts (cross-color and dot crawl) due to the imperfect decoders implemented in analog television sets. The advent of digital technologies in the 1990s allowed digital comb filters to be built into consumer television sets that for the first time extracted and displayed the full quality of the NTSC signal while effectively eliminating the artifacts. Ironically, these television sets became commercially available just as NTSC broadcast was being supplanted by digital cable and satellite delivery systems.

When considering the color space for digital cinema, these legacy systems were examined for their application. Obviously, the simplest approach, and the one most easily implemented with available technology, would have been to use the color television color space or to extend it. In fact, electronic cinema demonstrations with television projectors were conducted as far back as 1940.

In the late 1980s, Sony and other proponents of HDTV (high definition television) demonstrated electronic projection on small (20 foot wide) screens. However, the CRT projection technology was severely limited both in brightness and contrast ratio, and clearly was not ready for cinema applications. The GE Eidophor™ light valve technology, with a Xenon light source, was capable of lighting up large screens, but its complexity and cost ruled it out.

In 1997, Texas Instruments (TI) demonstrated a prototype DLP® (digital light processing) projector that used digital micro-mirror devices (DMDs) to modulate a Xenon light source with both high brightness and high contrast. These first demos caught the attention of Hollywood studio experts, who saw the promise of a digital technology that could someday replace film. Compared to a motion picture film print, this early DLP® projector prototype lacked resolution, contrast and color gamut, and the engineers at TI were sent back to the labs to work on improvements. The story of this work and the development of DLP Cinema® technology will be covered in a case study in Chapter 8.

Since the DLP® projection technology had been developed for graphics and video sources for such applications as business presentations and the event/staging market, the beam-splitting color prisms had been designed for video color space. In the initial tests in Hollywood, it became clear that this was not a large enough color space to match the gamut of a motion picture film print.

Based on measurements and extensive testing with colorists and cinematographers, the engineers at Texas Instruments used trim filters to narrow the response of the red, green and blue channels of the projector and expand its gamut substantially in red and green in order to more closely match film. It helped that the DLP® projectors used the same Xenon lamps as traditional film projectors, with a stable and continuous spectral output. However, trimming the color spectrum of the red and green channels traded off light output, so additional work had to be done to make the illumination system more efficient. This was coupled with parallel work to increase the resolution and contrast of the DMD devices.

The resulting improvements in color gamut, resolution and contrast were introduced to the industry in 1999 as part of the DLP Cinema® product specification. The DLP Cinema® color gamut is compared to that of Rec 709 (HDTV) and print film in Figure 3.2. The DLP Cinema gamut is expanded significantly beyond that of HDTV (CCIR 709) and encompasses most of the print film color gamut, except for deep cyans and magentas. The magenta colors do not occur in nature, but the deep cyans can be present in deep blue skies and emerald waters in tropical climates. In over 5 years of experience, this limitation has rarely been a problem. At the same time, DLP Cinema projectors are capable of producing much brighter primary colors (blues, greens and reds) than film.

These performance differences can be traced to the fundamental design of the two imaging systems. Film is strong in the subtractive colors, since its image is made up of combinations of cyan, magenta and yellow dyes, so a dark cyan or magenta produces the most saturated color. Digital projectors, on the other hand, work on an additive color basis, and produce the most saturated colors when its red, green or blue primaries are fully modulated.

So an obvious approach to digital cinema would have been to adopt the DLP Cinema® primaries and the corresponding color gamut, since it had been proven over five years of experience, including the release of over 150 feature films (at the time of this writing). But the studios and the creative community wanted more than that. Before we discuss the options that were considered, let's review the requirements that were identified by Digital Cinema Initiatives (DCI), the

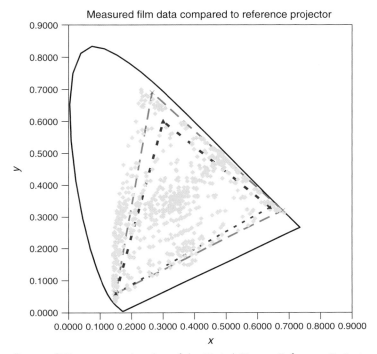

Figure 3-2. Color Gamut of Film compared to that of the Digital Cinema Reference Projector and ITU Rec. 709. A series of measured film samples are shown in the pastel green color, with the Reference Projector gamut shown by the dashed red line, and the ITU Rec. 709 gamut shown by the dashed blue line.

consortium established by the major Hollywood studios to develop a consensus specification for digital cinema.

The fundamental requirements that apply to the color of the projected digital cinema master can be extracted from the DCI Specification, Version 1.0 (page 3).

This led to the consideration of two options in addition to the DLP Cinema® color gamut. These additional options included a wider-gamut RGB space that encompassed all film colors and a parametric RGB encoding that carried the primaries of the reference projector as metadata.

In standard color science terminology, these three options are all output-referred image states. Since the objective of digital cinema distribution was to encode the color of the finished picture, including all of its creative color manipulations as displayed in the mastering suite, this was the obvious choice. Scene-referred color encoding would be more appropriate for image origination because it represents the color of the original scene. However, realistic or accurate color reproduction is not the principle goal of movie-making; rather it is the faithful reproduction of the creative

Quality	Better than a traditional 35 mm Answer Print.
Standards	Based on global standards that are embraced around the world so that content can be distributed and played anywhere in the world as can be done today with a 35 mm film print.
Reasonable Cost	The system specification should be chosen so that capital equipment and operational costs are reasonable and exploit, as much as possible, the economies of scale associated with equipment and technology in use in other industries.
Upgradeable	The hardware and software used in the system should be easily upgraded as advances in technology are made.
Backward Compatibility	New content at higher resolution or color space can be played out on a projection system that meets the baseline implementation.

Table 3-A.   DCI Requirements that apply to Color.

intent of the director and cinematographer, and their creative intent often includes intentional modifications to the color of the original scene in order to better convey the story and its emotional context. Although this may sound like semantics, image creation involves more than just recording or capturing the original scene.

An input-referred image state could also have been used, incorporating the characteristics of the original negative film or digital camera that was used to capture the scene. However, this state also excludes the creative intent, so it was likewise rejected as inappropriate for digital cinema distribution.

Furthermore, since cinema images are viewed in a dark surround, the eye's adaptation is very different from the observation of the original scene in its native environment. Generally speaking the contrast of a picture must be increased by approximately 50% to compensate for the dark surround viewing condition. This rendering for dark surround viewing is included in the output-referred image state.

Although based on practical experience and a proven implementation, the DLP Cinema® color primaries and associated gamut were not an acceptable solution because they did not provide for future improvements in display technology. Furthermore, these primaries were based on a particular implementation, rather than an internationally recognized standard. Finally, DLP Cinema® did not fully encompass the color gamut of print film, and (some might argue) did not fully meet the fundamental requirement of being better than a traditional 35 mm answer print.

As the SMPTE DC28 color ad hoc group explored options, there were many suggestions for a wider color gamut, some designed to use available laser light sources and others pushed out just wide enough to cover the full film gamut. However, there was much debate without a strong consensus on which set of wide gamut primaries to pick.

An alternative suggestion was made that seemed to combine the best of both worlds—Parametric RGB encoding. Basically, with Parametric RGB, the color primaries of the reference projector used in mastering would be sent with the encoded picture, and this metadata could be used by the cinema projector to determine if the colors were within its native gamut, and make a decision as to whether to map out of gamut colors. This approach allows the creative decision makers to embrace new wider-gamut projectors as they become commercially available, providing the required extensibility as well as a means for displaying these masters on first generation projectors (backward-compatibility).

Parametric RGB encoding intrinsically supports the DLP Cinema® primaries and color gamut—these are simply one set of parameters. Therefore, it would require no changes to existing products or to the installed base of first generation DLP Cinema® projectors. However, Parametric RGB encoding relies on metadata, and if the metadata is lost or incorrectly interpreted the color of the displayed picture would be ambiguous and could be impaired if the right presentation choices were not made. So, this approach is not robust.

At some point in the discussions, it was pointed out that rather than argue over which set of wide gamut color primaries to use, the group could just select the widest gamut set—the CIE 1931 color primaries. These three primaries are the basis of an international color standard that has stood the test of time, is the basis of all colorimetric measurement, and is widely used for color calibration in many industries. XYZ color encoding, as defined by the CIE 1931 Color Standard, met all of the DCI requirements. It provided no limits on future improvements since it enclosed all colors within the visual spectrum, while being compatible with today's products. And it did not rely on metadata - the XYZ colorimetric specification is completely deterministic. Another nice benefit is that the luminance information is directly accessible in the Y channel. Figure 3.3 shows the DLP Cinema primaries and the XYZ primaries, compared to the film gamut. Since the X, Y and Z primaries fall outside of the visible spectrum, they are not real primaries, but virtual primaries.

After some investigation and practical demonstrations, it was determined that XYZ color encoding could be implemented as a small extension to the existing mastering process and a small change to existing DLP Cinema projectors. For RGB-based color correction equipment and mastering, the only additional step required to convert the data to $X'Y'Z'$ is to linearize the RGB signal, apply a 3×3 matrix, and then gamma-encode the result. For data-based workflows, this can easily be accomplished in a batch software operation using commercially available tools such as Shake™. For hardware color correctors used in 2K workflows, the manufacturer would have to add an output color conversion, in most cases a simple matter of a new software release.

The only remaining concern was whether the inefficiencies of wide-gamut XYZ color encoding would result in scaling and quantization losses that would introduce picture impairments, or conversely would require too many bits to be practically implemented. The Barten model of the contrast sensitivity function of the Human Visual System (HVS) suggested that more than 10 bits,

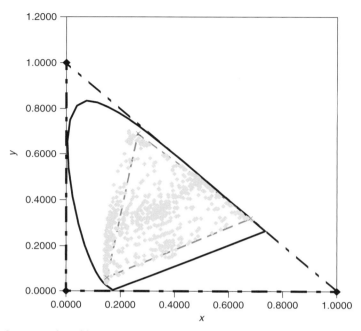

Figure 3-3. Color Gamut Enclosed by *XYZ* (dashed black line), compared to color gamut of the Digital Cinema Reference Projector (dashed red line) and the color gamut of film (pastel green).

Criteria	RGB DLP	X'Y'Z'	Parametric RGB
Coding Efficiency	All code values used	Less Efficient	All code values used
Device independence	No	Explicit	Thru metadata
Gamut used (region of interest)	Explicit	Metadata for gamut mapping	Explicit
Cinema equipment impact	None	Projector matrix	Projector matrix
Mastering equipment impact	None	Color correction matrix	None
Extensibility	No	Explicit	Thru metadata
Backward compatibility	No	Explicit	Thru metadata
Simplicity/Robustness	Locked down	Fully defined	Requires metadata
Basis on existing standards	709 extended	CIE 1931	None
Compression implications	Transform req'd	Y isolated	Transform req'd
Cost implications	None	Small/None	Small/None

Table 3-B. The RGB DLP, *X'Y'Z'* and Parameteric RGB color space options are compared versus key considerations in this table. A green background implies that the requirement is met, red that it is precluded, and yellow signifies that it is met, but with more complicated implementation.

but less than 12 bits, were required to encode the contrast range and luminance levels required for cinema presentation, so long as the signal was gamma-encoded to distribute the bits efficiently. However, this model was based on a series of experiments in other viewing conditions and had never been verified under cinema viewing conditions. A practical experiment was designed to verify that the Barten model applied to cinema—this will be discussed in detail in Chapter 4. Since most existing equipment processes 12 or 16 bit internally and the existing dual-link HD-SDI interface supports 12 bits per color, the implementation hurdles are small. It will also be shown that the bit efficiency is not a critical consideration.

There was some resistance to XYZ color encoding based on the lack of experience in the motion picture or television industries. Some were worried that it might not compress efficiently. At that point, DCI had yet to select the compression technology for digital cinema distribution— JPEG2000 would be specified later—but this was deemed a small risk. In the past couple of years, practical tests have shown that the color transformations can be implemented easily and transparently by multiple parties working independently from the draft SMPTE DC28 documents and that 12 bits are sufficient (no artifacts have been introduced in the process). Further, practical compression tests have also shown that XYZ color components can be compressed as efficiently as RGB. With the encoding and release of several movies in XYZ format (at the time of this writing), these fears have been assuaged.

It is useful to take a short detour and describe the basis for XYZ color encoding, the CIE (Commission Internationale de l'Eclairage) 1931 Standard Colorimetric Observer. The CIE 1931 Standard Colorimetric Observer was based on two experiments that empirically defined a standard for human vision based on trichromatic (three color) matching. As shown in Figure 3.4, an observer was asked to match a color, C, by adjusting the intensities of an additive red, green and blue source. These initial experiments were conducted by J. Guild at the UK's National Physical Laboratory at Teddington, using a tungsten lamp and color filters, and by W.D. Wright, at Imperial College in Kensington, using monochromatic bands of light isolated by a series of prisms.

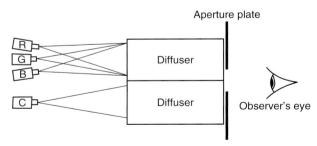

Figure 3-4. Trichromatic Matching (Source: R.W.B. Hunt, "Measuring Color", Third Edition, Fountain Press, England, © 1998, p. 38.)

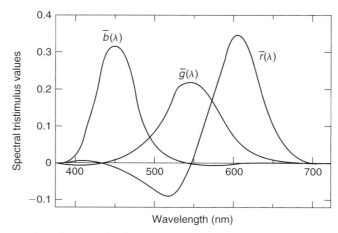

Figure 3-5. The color matching functions for the CIE 1931 Standard Colorimetric Observer. (Source: R.W.B. Hunt, "Measuring Color", Third Edition, Fountain Press, England, © 1998, p. 43.)

To combine and calibrate the data, each set was transformed mathematically to the following monochromatic matching stimuli: 700 nm red, 546.1 nm green and 435.8 nm blue. The green and blue stimuli were chosen to coincide with prominent mercury discharge lines to facilitate calibration. The red stimulus was selected from the long wavelength part of the spectrum where changes vary slowly with wavelength to reduce calibration errors. For convenience the red, green and blue stimuli were scaled so that equal amounts of red, green and blue resulted in a white color. The amounts of these three matching stimuli, expressed in these scaled units, are known as tristimulus values.

The results of these experiments were Color Matching Functions (CMF) for the CIE 1931 Standard Colorimetric Observer, as shown in Figure 3.5. These curves are designated by $\bar{r}(\lambda)$, $\bar{g}(\lambda)$ and $\bar{b}(\lambda)$. Each curve shows the amount of its respective color required to produce a match for each wavelength of the spectrum. Note that the r-bar (lambda) curve has a substantial negative value in the green to blue part of the spectrum, while the others also show small negative excursions. This negative contribution was not created by adding "negative" red light, rather by adding this amount of red to the test color in the experiment in order to match the color. It should also be noted that the light of 700 nm is matched by the red stimuli only, 546.1 nm by green only and 435.8 nm by blue only, as expected. By selecting other monochromatic stimuli, one can move these zero intersections to different wavelengths, but the color matching functions will still have negative excursions since the responses of the red and blue cones overlap that of the green cones, making it impossible to independently stimulate only the green cones.

Since color matches have been proven to be additive (see Grassmann's Laws), these color matching functions can be used as weighting functions to determine the amounts of R, G, and B required to match any color of any spectral composition, if that spectrum can be decomposed into equal intervals of 5 or 10 nm. These tristimulus values are defined as:

$$R \equiv k(P_1\overline{r}_1 + P_2\overline{r}_2 + P_3\overline{r}_3 + \cdots)$$
$$G = k(P_1\overline{g}_1 + P_2\overline{g}_2 + P_3\overline{g}_3 + \cdots)$$
$$B = k(P_1\overline{b}_1 + P_2\overline{b}_2 + P_3\overline{b}_3 + \cdots)$$

And the luminance of the resulting color is given by:

$$L = 1.0000\ R + 4.5907\ G + 0.0601\ B$$

The constant k is chosen so that if P is watts per steradian per square meter, L is in candelas per square meter (cd/m^2).

The values of R, G, and B as defined above provided a precise system of color specification based on human visual experiments that could be used to calculate color tristimulus values from spectral data of color stimuli. However, the CIE wanted to avoid negative numbers in the color specifications to make the implementation simpler, so they algebraically scaled the three R, G and B tristimulus values to create a new set of tristimulus values, X, Y and Z, using the following equations:

$$X = 0.49\ R + 0.31\ G + 0.20\ B$$
$$Y = 0.17697\ R + 0.81240\ G + 0.01063\ B$$
$$Z = 0.00\ R + 0.01\ G + 0.99\ B$$

The coefficients in these equations were chosen carefully so that X, Y, and Z would always be positive for all colors.

The coefficients of the Y channel were chosen such that they are in the same ratios as the luminances of the matching R, G and B stimuli, which means that the value Y is proportional to the CIE 1924 photopic luminous efficiency function, V(λ), commonly called luminance. And since the coefficients of each equation sum to unity, the equal energy stimulus is represented by R = G = B, and also by X = Y = Z.

The CIE color matching functions are then defined by the following equations:

$$\overline{x}(\lambda) = 0.49\ \overline{r}(\lambda) + 0.31\ \overline{g}(\lambda) + 0.20\ \overline{b}(\lambda)$$
$$\overline{y}(\lambda) = 0.17697\ \overline{r}(\lambda) + 0.81240\ \overline{g}(\lambda) + 0.01063\ \overline{b}(\lambda)$$
$$\overline{z}(\lambda) = 0.00\ \overline{r}(\lambda) + 0.01\ \overline{g}(\lambda) + 0.99\ \overline{b}(\lambda)$$

These color matching functions form the basis of the CIE 1931 Standard Colorimetric Observer and are shown in Figure 3.6, and are generally referred to as the 2° observer, since the color matching fields represented a 2° field of view. As expected, these color matching functions have no negative excursions.

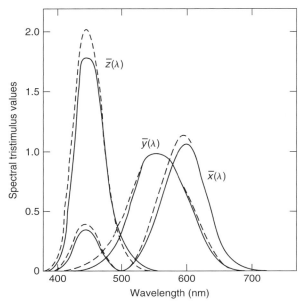

Figure 3-6. The CIE x, y and z color matching functions for the 1931 Standard Colorimetric Observer (solid lines) and for the 1964 Supplementary Standard Colorimetric Observer (dashed lines). (Source: R.W.B. Hunt, "Measuring Color", Third Edition, Fountain Press, England, © 1998, p. 47.)

Like before, the $\bar{x}(\lambda)$, $\bar{y}(\lambda)$, and $\bar{z}(\lambda)$ functions can be used as weighting functions to calculate X, Y and Z tristimulus values directly from spectral power data using the following formulae:

$$X \equiv K(P_1\bar{x}_1(l) + P_2\bar{x}_2(l) + P_3\bar{x}_3(l) + \cdots)$$
$$Y = K(P_1\bar{y}_1(l) + P_2\bar{y}_2(l) + P_3\bar{y}_3(l) + \cdots)$$
$$Z = K(P_1\bar{z}_1(l) + P_2\bar{z}_2(l) + P_3\bar{z}_3(l) + \cdots)$$

If P is in watts per steradian per square meter and K is set to 683, then Y is the luminance in candelas per square meter (cd/m^2).

IS THE 1931 CIE STANDARD OBSERVER STILL VALID?

Some have questioned whether the initial experiments included enough observers, whether these observers are still representative of normal human vision, and whether the derived color matching functions have sufficient precision. The initial experiments included only 17 observers, and therefore represent the average color matching properties of 17 English observers from 1931.

In 1951, Judd proposed a revision to the 1931 CIE standard observer that increased the response at low wavelengths to compensate for measurement errors. In the 1950's, Stiles was encouraged by the CIE Colorimetry Committee to perform a new test to re-determine the color matching functions. In a 1955 report, Stiles noted some differences between the new data and the 1931 CIE standard observer, but concluded that these differences were not large enough to require a change.

Since that time, others have repeated the test and validated the early results, concluding that the CIE Standard Observer adequately represents normal human vision in 2° fields, while acknowledging that observers vary significantly and that many physical factors affect human vision, including genetic factors affecting eye pigmentation and age.

However, color matches made with a 2° field of view may not remain matches as the field of view is increased, because the spectral properties of the retina vary from one point to another. In 1964, the CIE recommended a supplementary set of color matching functions based on an experiment with a 10° field of view. These CMFs, while similar in shape, have large enough differences to be significant. These new color matching functions, $\overline{x}_{10}(\lambda)$, $\overline{y}_{10}(\lambda)$, and $\overline{z}_{10}(\lambda)$, define the CIE 1964 Supplementary Standard Colorimetric Observer. Unlike , $\overline{y}(\lambda)$ the $\overline{y}_{10}(\lambda)$ function has no photometric significance. In fact, photometric measures are not additive in 10° fields like they are with 2° fields.

Although X, Y and Z color matching functions are the basis of standard colorimetric measurements, most of these measurements are reported in terms of luminance (Y) and chromaticities, x and y. These color values are obtained with a simple algebraic transform from X, Y and Z.

$$X = X/(X + Y + Z)$$
$$y = Z/(X + Y + Z)$$
$$Y = Y$$

And, since $x + y + z = 1$, the value of z is derived simply:

$$Z = 1 - x - y$$

Using the customary x, y chromaticity diagram in Figure 3.7, the color gamut for the digital cinema reference projector is shown, compared to ITU Rec. 709 (HDTV) and the visible spectrum. A curve is also shown for Daylight illuminants with points identified for D55, and D65.

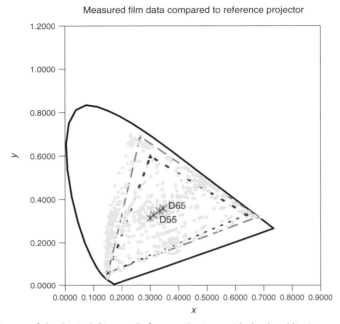

Figure 3-7. Color Gamut of the Digital Cinema Reference Projector (dashed red line), compared to film samples (pastel green) and HDTV (dashed blue line). The boundaries of the visible spectrum is shown by the solid black horseshoe. Several points on the daylight illuminant curve are shown, with D55 and D65 labelled.

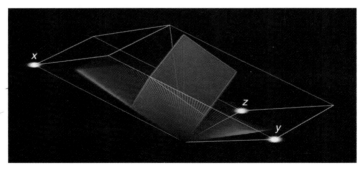

Figure 3-8. Three Dimensional Color Plot of *XYZ* color space, showing the outlines of the visible spectrum and the box inclosed by the additive primaries of the Digital Cinema Reference projector (rendering courtesy of Jeremy Selan and George Joblove of Sony Pictures Imageworks).

Since color has three dimensions, it is instructive to look at a volumetric color gamut. Figure 3.8 shows a three dimensional color space plot for XYZ color space, showing the visible spectrum and the additive RGB Digital Cinema Reference Projector.[1]

---

1. J. Selan and G. Joblove, Sony Imageworks, © 2004.

4
Transfer Function

An important characteristic of any digital imaging system is the transfer function that defines the relationship between its code values and the displayed picture. This chapter will review the background that led to the specification of a non-linear encoding transfer function for digital cinema distribution that is based on a power law with a gamma of 1/2.6.

The CIE XYZ tristimulus values are calculated with a normalizing constant (52.37) that sets the Y tristimulus value equal to the relative luminance in cd/m² above black, and both the X and Z values are multiplied by the same constant. With this specification of the color, the following equations define the encoding transfer function where X, Y, Z are the tristimulus values above black.

$$CV_{X'} = INT\left[4095 \times \left(\frac{X}{52.37}\right)^{1/2.6}\right] \tag{1}$$

$$CV_{Y''} = INT\left[4095 \times \left(\frac{Y}{52.37}\right)^{1/2.6}\right] \tag{2}$$

$$CV_{Z'} = INT\left[4095 \times \left(\frac{Z}{52.37}\right)^{1/2.6}\right] \tag{3}$$

Why was the gamma (power law) of 1/2.6 selected? Why was twelve bits (4096 discrete code values) selected to quantize the signal range? To answer these questions, we need to consider the contrast sensitivity of the human visual system.

XYZ colorimetry is linear by definition, representing luminance levels that are proportional to the light on the screen. Linear light encoding is convenient for image synthesis and computer graphics because the underlying physics and shading models are linear. However, linear encoding does not match the response of the human visual system, which is approximately logarithmic in nature. So, more bits are required to produce smooth, contour-free pictures in a linear model compared to a logarithmic or gamma-encoded representation. Contouring occurs when a step size of one code value is visible, as illustrated in Figure 4.1. To eliminate contouring, the image must be digitized at a sufficient bit depth so that each bit represents a luminance change that is below the threshold of visibility.

In vision research, the most important parameter that affects contouring is the Contrast Sensitivity Function (CSF). The CSF is inversely proportional to the minimum visible modulation, which for a sinusoidal signal is defined as

$$m = \frac{L_{high} - L_{low}}{(L_{high} + L_{low})} = \frac{\Delta L}{2 \times L_{average}}$$

where L_{high} and L_{low} are the maximum and minimum luminance in the sine wave, ΔL is the difference between L_{high} and L_{low}, and $L_{average}$ is the average of L_{high} and L_{low}.

Barten has defined a model of the contrast sensitivity function of the human eye, which predicts the visual modulation threshold of sine waves as a function of a large number of variables. The visual modulation threshold as a function of luminance is shown in Figure 4.1. The luminance range used for the projection of motion pictures in a theater covers from the peak white of about 50 cd/m^2 to as low as 0.005 cd/m^2, covering a 10,000:1 luminance range. Because the human visual modulation threshold is curved on Figure 4.2 over this luminance range, there is no simple equation that fits this curve.

The most efficient equation is one that matches as closely as possible the shape of the human visual modulation threshold curve in Figure 4.2. A power law expression is a reasonable, yet simple fit for the visual modulation threshold. It produces an encoding equation of the form

$$CV = CV_{max} \times \left(\frac{L}{P}\right)^{1/m} \tag{4}$$

(a)

(b)

Figure 4-1a and 4-1b. The effect of limited bit depth is to introduce quantizing errors that result in visible banding in shaded areas of an image. With adequate bit depth (Figure 4.1a), the sky appears smoothly shaded. Inadequate bit depth (Figure 4.1b) results in banding artifacts.

with a corresponding decoding equation of the form

$$L = P \times \left(\frac{CV}{CV_{max}} \right)^{n} \tag{5}$$

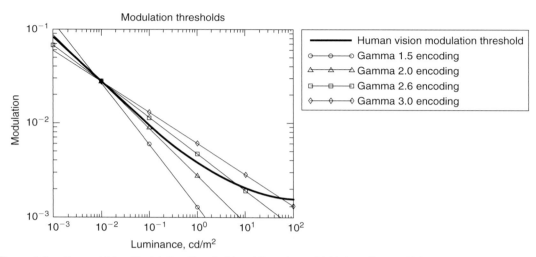

Figure 4-2. Human Vision Modulation Threshold and Equations with Various Gamma Values.

In these equations CV_{max} is

$$CV_{max} = 2^b - 1 \tag{6}$$

where b is the bit depth of the encoding.

In the general case, the encoding exponent is 1/m and the decoding exponent is n. Because the encoding is an output referred encoding and the final color is rendered or "baked into" the Digital Cinema Distribution Master (DCDM) code values, the exponent in the decoding equation has to be the inverse of the exponent in the encoding equation. This means m must equal n and the Greek letter gamma, γ, is used as the symbol. If m does not equal n, the encoding and decoding operations will produce a change in the contrast of the images and this was not desired.

The next step is to select the value of gamma. There are two reasons for choosing 2.6 as the value of γ in the exponents. The first reason is quite simple: DLP Cinema® projectors had been using that value for several years with success. This gamma was selected through practical testing in mastering suites to determine which projection display gamma worked best with existing telecine and color correction equipment. The colorist was asked to grade a variety of scenes to match a projected color print film, and practical testing determined that this match-grading process was easiest when the projector's display gamma was set to 2.6.

The second reason is that a gamma of 2.6 matches the human visual modulation curve in Figure 4.2 relatively well. Figure 1 shows curves for equations with gamma values of 1.5, 2.0, 2.6, and 3.0.

These curves have been matched at a luminance of 0.01 cd/m^2 so that a visual comparison among the curves can be easily made. Although these curves can be shifted left or right to optimize the fit of the curve to the human visual modulation threshold curve, the slope of the curves is determined by the gamma value. Clearly the 1.5 and 2.0 gamma curves have a slope that is too steep and the 3.0 gamma curve has a slope that is too shallow. Therefore, although there may be other gamma values near 2.6 that are equally good fits, it was decided to use a gamma value of 2.6. Because the exact shape and position of the human visual modulation threshold curve changes as a function of a number of variables, there is no sense in trying to find the gamma value that mathematically fits the visual curve.

12-bit Encoding

The human visual modulation threshold curve can also be used to determine the bit depth of the encoding. From the general decoding equation, Equation 5, the luminance that corresponds to each code value can be calculated. A value of P of 48 cd/m^2 was used at this time because it had been decided that the luminance of the white would be 48 cd/m^2, but the final answer on bit depth is only weakly dependent on the value of P. The variable CV_{max} is directly related to the bit depth of the encoding as shown in equation 6.

$$CV_{max} = 2^n - 1 \qquad\qquad (6)$$

where n is the bit depth of the encoding. For compatibility with existing digital imaging and computing systems, it makes sense to consider only even numbers of bits for the encoding. Given this, it is relatively easy to calculate the luminance for every code value for a specific bit depth. Because the minimum ΔL is the change in luminance when the code value is changed by one, the modulation of a specific bit depth encoding can be calculated for all luminance values using Equation 1. Figure 4.3 shows the human visual modulation threshold curve and the curves for 8, 10, 12, and 14-bit encoding. In Figure 4.3, patterns above or to the right of the human vision modulation threshold curve can be seen and patterns below or to the left of the curve cannot be seen. Because this curve has been calculated for optimum visibility of the sine wave patterns, this represents the limiting case.

There are a number of factors that can make a pattern invisible even though it may lie above the human vision modulation threshold curve. For example, noise or grain in an image will shift the threshold curve up and to the right. However, computer generated animation can be produced with no noise and a viable digital cinema distribution standard must obviously support these movies too. Based on Figure 4.2, it appears that 8-bit encoding has too few bits, 12-bit encoding (or higher) has more bits than are needed to avoid any bit depth related image artifacts), while 10-bit encoding looks like it has slightly too few bits and 11 bits would be sufficient if we were willing to use an odd number of bits.

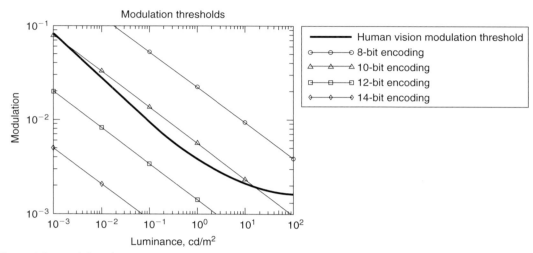

Figure 4-3. Visibility of 8-, 10-, 12-, and 14-bit encoding.

Figure 4.3 is based on calculations only. Certainly there are good experiments behind the human visual modulation threshold curve, but these experiments were not conducted in cinema viewing conditions, and that curve is dependent on a general model with a large number of variables. Because of the increased cost and the time to upgrade equipment to 12-bit image processing, there was a considerable reluctance to accept the 12-bit encoding answer without doing some verification experiments in a theater environment with D-Cinema projection. Therefore, an experiment was designed and conducted to determine if people could see patterns encoded with a bit depth of 10 and how that compared with patterns encoded with a bit depth of 12. These results have been described in detail in a paper published in the SMPTE Journal[1].

Using a digital projector, square wave patterns were projected onto the screen in a dark theater[2]. The observers, who were volunteers from the SMPTE DC28 meetings, studio employees, cinematographers, a few film school students, and some untrained recruits off the street, were seated in groups that were located at four different distances from the screen. The square waves were oriented either vertically or horizontally. The observers were asked to identify the orientation of the square waves. There were three luminance levels at which the experiment was run, there were six modulation levels shown to the observers at each luminance level, and there were six repetitions of each luminance-modulation combination. For each luminance level and each observer,

1. M. Cowan, G. Kennel, T. Maier and B. Walker, "Contrast Sensitivity Experiment to Determine the Bit Depth for Digital Cinema", SMPTE Journal 113:9, September 2004.
2. Tests were performed at the Digital Cinema Lab, operated by the USC Entertainment Technology Center.

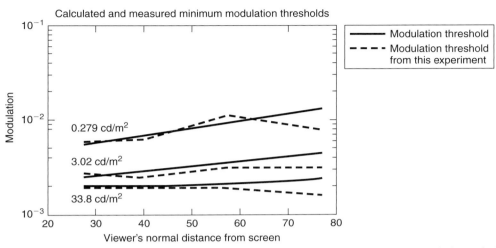

Figure 4-4. A Comparison of the Modulation Thresholds Determined in the Theater and the Calculated Modulation Thresholds.

a plot was made of each observer's fraction of the orientations identified correctly. The observer's modulation threshold is the modulation at which that observer correctly identified 75% of the orientations correctly. Figure 4.4 shows a comparison of the average threshold modulation of each of the groups of observers (grouped by distance from the screen in feet) and the calculated human visual modulation threshold.

In Figure 4.4 the calculated threshold varies as a function of distance due to the varying field of view and the varying frequency of the square waves as seen by the observer. Even though the observers farthest from the screen consistently had a lower modulation threshold than calculated by the Barten model, the results are in excellent agreement with the calculations. This gives strong support to the validity of the use of the calculated human visual modulation threshold for determining the bit depth needed for digital cinema encoding.

The results in Figure 4.4 show the averages of groups of observers, but do not give any information on the distribution of the results around each average. Figures 4.5, 4.6, and 4.7 show cumulative frequency histograms of the observers' responses as a function of modulation threshold.

Figures 4.5, 4.6 and 4.7 give an indication of the distribution of the observers' thresholds around the averages. Also shown in Figures 4.5, 4.6 and 4.7 are the modulations of 10, 11, and 12-bit encoding using equations similar to Equations 1–3, but differing in that the 4095 constant, which is needed for 12-bit encoding, was changed to 1023 and 2047 for 10-bit and 11-bit encoding calculations, respectively. The results shown here are slightly different from those in the SMPTE

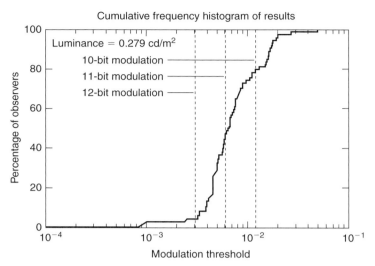

Figure 4-5. Cumulative Frequency Histogram for the Results Obtained at an Average Luminance of 0.279 cd/m².

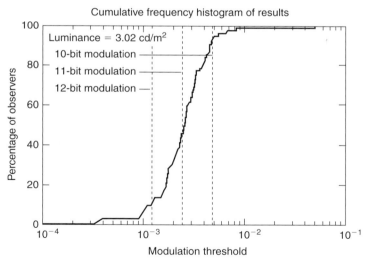

Figure 4-6. Cumulative Frequency Histogram for the Results Obtained at an Average Luminance of 3.02 cd/m².

Journal article because the constant 52.37 in Equations 1–6 was 41.11 at the time of that work. The change is very small and does not alter the conclusions. Table 4-A shows the percentage of observers who correctly identified the orientation of the square waves at the 50% confidence level as a function of the luminance and bit depth.

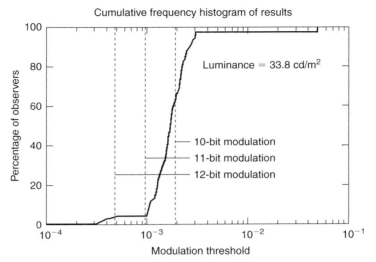

Figure 4-7. Cumulative Frequency Histogram for the Results Obtained at an Average Luminance of 33.8 cd/m^2.

Luminance cd/m^2	Bit Depth		
	10 bits	11 bits	12 bits
0.279	80%	47%	4%
3.02	92%	46%	9%
33.8	62%	4%	4%

Table 4-A. Percentage of Observers Who Correctly Identifed the Orientation of the Square Waves.

Table 4-A shows that with 10-bit or 11-bit encoding a sizeable number of the observers could see the square waves, but with 12-bit encoding only a few observers will see the square waves. The visibility of the square waves is an indication of whether observers will observe contouring in an image. This was a much more critical test than the observation of contouring in a typical image because here there were 13 square waves in a pattern, which means 27 luminance transitions, and in a shaded image with contouring, there is one luminance transition, which is in effect one-half of a square wave. Published results and the results of calculations of the human vision modulation threshold indicate that the modulation threshold when there is only one square wave is about ten times higher than when there are 13 square waves. Therefore, although this experiment indicates that a few observers will be able to identify the orientation of the square waves with 12-bit encoding, no observers are expected to see contouring in pictures with 12-bit encoding.

Although this experiment demonstrates that the minimum one code value change that cannot be seen is a bit depth of 12-bits, the digital projectors in use today are being fed an 8-bit signal compressed at 4:2:0. Because of the nature of the encoding equation, Equations 1–3 , the modulation encoded by a one code value change when the bit depth decreases by one bit changes by a factor of 2. This can be seen in Figure 3 where 10-bit and 12-bit encoding equations are compared. The modulation changes as the luminance changes, but the ratio of the modulation of the 10-bit encoding to the modulation of the 12-bit encoding is a constant 4.0 due to the fact that the encoding changed by 2 bits. So one might ask how images encoded in 8 bits can perform acceptably today, if 12-bit encoding is needed to encode luminance changes below the threshold of visibility. This is a change in modulation by a factor of 16 because the change in bit depth is 4 bits.

Because the modulation threshold will also be increased by any noise, dithering, or grain in the image, it is possible to see how the 8-bit current images can perform without significant contouring artifacts. This, then, raises the question as to whether 12-bit encoding is really needed to avoid the contouring artifact in real-world images. It can be demonstrated that widely available 10-bit images, particularly when they include film grain or a small amount of masking noise perform adequately in digital cinema display. It is important to note that the DCI specifications do not define the characteristics of the source image, only those of the digital cinema distribution master (DCDM). In this as in many other ways, the DCI specifications provide head-room to support further improvements in image capture or generation.

The above calculations and experiment demonstrate that 11 or 12 bits are needed to encode the luminance channel without contouring. Whether the luminance is carried in the Y' channel as is done in the DCDM encoding or in the R', G', and B' channels with another set of primaries, the neutral scale must be encoded with 12 bits. So it is the neutral scale encoding that defines the need for 12-bit encoding.

Early in the discussions of the encoding primaries, there was considerable attention paid to the efficiency of the encoding, which varied as a function of the primaries chosen. The wide gamut X'Y'Z' encoding is a particularly inefficient encoding, which means there are a very large number of sets of X'Y'Z' values that lie outside the spectral locus, and are therefore wasted. However, it is now clear that the discussion of encoding efficiency was a distraction if no more than 12-bits per channel are needed for the encoding of the neutral scale.

The best estimates of the number of colors that a person can differentiate are 2 million to 10 million. 12-bit encoding allows the encoding of roughly 64 billion colors. Therefore, with a 12-bit encoding system, the encoding efficiency has to be at best about 0.003%. If 12-bit encoding of the neutral scale is sufficient to avoid contouring in luminance, there is a need for only 4096 encoded luminance values along the neutral scale.

HOW DOES VIDEO GET AWAY WITH ONLY 8 OR 10 BITS?

Today's standards for digital television production support only 10 bits. In fact, early professional digital video equipment supported only 8 bits. Similarly, MPEG-2 digital broadcast standards and the common Digital Video Interface (DVI) for home video equipment support only 8 bits. Why does this work?

First of all, a skilled observer can easily spot contouring artifacts with broadcast MPEG-2 encoded content, but home video systems are not held to the same high (artifact-free) standard as digital cinema. Today, minimizing the equipment cost is more important than pristine picture quality in consumer applications.

With professional video equipment, the move from 8 bits to 10 bits in the early 1990's resulted in a huge improvement in picture quality and essentially eliminated contouring artifacts from any image source with a little bit of masking noise, whether these pictures came from television cameras or digitized film. In computer generated graphics or animation, it is a common practice to either inject a little noise or dither the least significant bit (LSB) in the output to effectively mask contouring artifacts.

But it is also important to keep in mind that the higher contrast of digital cinema images makes this presentation more demanding than that of a television display. So what's good enough for television is not necessarily good enough for cinema.

Full Range

The full range of the digital cinema signal is available for use. In other words, there are 4096 code values in each of the 12-bit X', Y' and Z' channels, and all of these are valid. Unlike digital television standards, there are no illegal code values. Utilization of the full range is consistent with common practice in computer-based visual effects and computer generated images, and was strongly promoted by advocates from this community.

However, this concept raised concerns with traditional television engineers and there was much discussion in early SMPTE DC28 committee meetings. Two principal concerns were identified. One, 10-bit digital television signals were defined with reference white at 940 and reference black at 64 code values that provided ample range for analog filter over (or under) shoots. Secondly, digital video interfaces reserved four code values at each end of the scale for other purposes.

Digital video standards were developed as an addition and compliment to analog broadcast standards and were required to be backward-compatible with existing analog video equipment. Establishing reference white and black levels and providing ample headroom for analog variations was a prudent practice to avoid clipping artifacts. But these constraints do no apply to digital cinema mastering or distribution, which is a purely digital process.

Today's digital cinema systems utilize the SMPTE 372 dual-link high definition serial digital interface (HD-SDI), and are subject to its reserved code values. In the 12-bit dual-link mode, this means that the lowest 0–15 code values and the upper 4080–4095 code values are reserved. When a full-range digital cinema signal is transported over a SMPTE 372 interface, any code values that fall under 15 or over 4080 are clipped to those code values. In practice, this is insignificant. At the low end, the gamma 2.6 display look-up table compresses output code values to zero below an input of 40 code values anyway. At the high end, 15 code values (out of 4095) represent a very small luminance change, and with the white point normalized to provide headroom for future adjustments, it is irrelevant today. This will be described next.

Normalization Factor for White Point

In Equations 1–3, it would seem that the constant that normalizes the XYZ variables should be the maximum luminance that can be encoded. Early in the development of the DCDM standard this was 48.00 cd/m^2 (14 ft L). So, where does the value of 52.37 come from? Because the SMPTE D-Cinema standards specify a maximum luminance of 48.00 cd/m^2, with a normalizing constant of 52.37, the maximum Y' code value that is allowed is 3960. However, because there is no limit on the X' and Z' values because they carry no luminance information, the maximum X' and Z' values are 4095. Some implementations or hardware, due to reserved code values, may set a lower maximum code value on X' and Z', but the reason for allowing them to have higher values than Y' still holds. The reason for the use of the 52.37 is that the gamut of the encoding space is increased and in particular there are more white point color temperatures along the CIE D-Illuminant line on a chromaticity diagram that can be encoded at the maximum luminance, 48.00 cd/m^2. The following calculations and plots will make this clearer.

If Equations 1–3 were to use a value of 48.00 as the normalizing constant, a luminance of 48.00 will be encoded any time the Y' code value is 4095. The encoding white point, which will be discussed in the section below and which is defined as the point where the code values are equal and at their maximum values, would be |4095 4095 4095|. The notation |X' Y' Z'| is used here to indicate the X'Y'Z' code values for one color. The XYZ luminance values corresponding to this color are |48 48 48|. The xy chromaticity coordinates corresponding to this color are |0.3333 0.3333 0.3333|. One of the encoding gamut boundaries at the maximum luminance and in the direction from the white point toward yellow (maximum values of X and Y) is defined by the set of values |4095 4095 B| where B is less than 4095. Likewise, another encoding gamut boundary at the maximum luminance and in the direction from the white point toward cyan (maximum values of Y and Z) is defined by the set of values |R 4095 4095| where R is less than 4095. Figure 4.8 shows the plane of maximum luminance that can be encoded using 48.00 as the normalizing constant. Figure 4.9 shows an

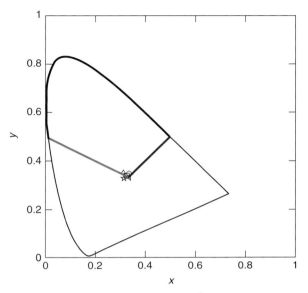

Figure 4-8. Encoded Gamut Boundary at a Luminance of 48 cd/m^2 and with a Normalizing Constant of 48.00.

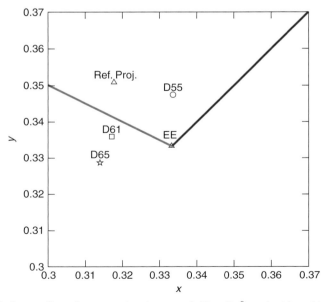

Figure 4-9. Encoded Gamut Boundary at a Luminance of 48 cd/m^2 and with a Normalizing Constant of 48.00 (Enlarged).

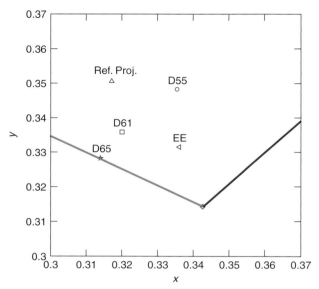

Figure 4-10.   Encoded Gamut Boundary at a Luminance of 48 cd/m² and with a Normalizing Constant of 52.37.

enlarged version of the same plot so that the area around the most common white points can be more clearly seen. In these figures, the area that can be encoded with real colors is above the dark red and blue lines and below the dark black line. Therefore it can be seen that with this normalizing constant, D55, the Equal Energy Point, and the Reference Projector white point can be encoded, but D61 and D65 cannot be encoded at 48 cd/m².

In order to provide headroom for possible changes in white point preference, the normalization factor was changed to allow the encoding of D65 at the maximum luminance of 48 cd/m². Using Equations 8 and 9 with 12-bit encoding, limiting the maximum luminance to 48 cd/m², and enclosing D65 in the encoded gamut, leads to the normalizing constant of 52.37. With this normalizing constant the gamut on the 48 cd/m² plane is shown in Figure 4.10. It can be seen that the D65 point is the point that forces the 52.37 constant because the D55 and the Equal Energy points are well inside the encoded gamut. The point where the red and blue lines meet in Figure 4.8 is at chromaticity coordinates |0.3429 0.3143|.

As is shown in Figure 4.11, the use of 52.37 as the normalizing constant has no significant effect on the visibility of contouring. The modulation for the 52.37 normalizing constant is not significantly different from the 48.00 normalizing constant.

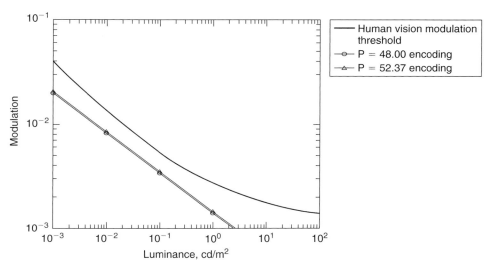

Figure 4-11. Encoding Modulation for a Normalizing Constant of 48.00 and 52.37 in the Encoding Equation.

White Points

In an additive imaging system the white point is commonly defined as the color (or chromaticity coordinates and luminance) that is produced when the system is sent the maximum RGB code values that it can accept. In some cases, for a variety of reasons, commonly because some code values are reserved, the maximum code values are somewhat less than the maximum as determined from the bit depth of the digital encoding. However, it is common to define the white point as coming from equal RGB code values. With this definition of the white point of a system and from Equations 1–3, the encoding white point for the DCDM system is the Equal Energy Point and the chromaticity coordinates of this point are |0.3333 0.3333|. The Equal Energy Point is shown on Figures 4.8–4.10 as the point labeled EE. The entire neutral scale, defined as the scale of grays from white to black with equal code values, falls at this same set of chromaticity coordinates.

In the DCI specifications and SMPTE Standard for Screen Luminance and Chromaticity, the white point is defined as having chromaticity coordinates |0.314 0.351| and is shown in Figures 4.8–4.10 as the point labeled Ref. Proj.. Clearly the white point for a properly set-up and calibrated digital projector does not have to be the same as the encoding white point. There was considerable discussion of what encoding white point to use, but the final decision was to use the Equal Energy Point because it simplified the implementation. Because there will always have to be a conversion from the encoding code values based on the encoding primaries, which define a device-independent system, to the projector code values based on the projector primaries, which define a device-dependent system, the encoding white point and the projector white point do not have to be the same. Because the color balance of any scene is set for artistic and aesthetic reasons, the color balance, including the white point, of any scene has to correspond to neither the encoding white point nor the projector white point.

There are two important considerations to remember concerning white points in the DCDM system. Firstly, the encoding white point is determined from the encoding Equations 1–3 because they define the relationship between colorimetric samples and the encoded code values. Secondly, the projector white point is defined by the proper set-up and calibration of a specific projector. If the projector is properly set up and the primaries and white point of that projector are known, the conversion between the encoded code values and the internal projector code values is relatively easy. The process by which this conversion is done will be described below.

Relative Luminance Encoding

In a dark theater there will be some light reflected onto the screen and back to the audience due to the lights required by building safety codes. In addition, if the code value 0 is sent to the projector, some light will fall on the screen from the projector even though code value 0 defines no light. This light, the light from the safety lights and the light from the projector when a code value 0 was sent, bounced off the screen will be called 'theater black' because it is the blackest black that can be measured off the screen in that theater with the projector turned on. In a dark theater, the theater black will not alter the white point because the white light out of the projector is so much brighter than the theater black.

The ratio of the white luminance to the theater black luminance is called the contrast ratio. If the chromaticity coordinates and luminance of the theater black were the same in all theaters over all time, there would not be a problem. However, review rooms typically have a lower theater black luminance than public cinemas, because they are subject to less stringent safety requirements. Also, manufacturers continue to improve the contrast ratio of their projector products. A higher contrast ratio (given the defined screen luminance level), results in a lower luminance of the theater black. Because review rooms are typically equipped with the best equipment available, they will most likely be capable of delivering blacker blacks.

If the encoding of the luminance in the DCDM represents the absolute luminance of the light reflected by the screen, then the encoding represents both the light from the projector with a code value greater than 0 plus the theater black. Also, code value 0 represents absolutely no light reflected from the screen.

Conversely, if the encoding of the luminance in the DCDM represents the relative luminance of the light reflected by the screen, where relative means the luminance above the theater black, then the encoding represents the light emitted by the projector when a code value greater than 0 is sent to the projector and reflected by the screen. Although this may sound like an encoding of the light emitted by the projector, it is not the light emitted by the projector because the screen has to be involved also – the light is measured as reflected off the screen. Therefore, with relative luminance the light must be measured with a meter pointed at the screen, not pointed directly at the projector. Also, code value 0 represents theater black reflected from the screen and this includes some contribution from the ambient light in the room.

In the limiting case in which the theater black XYZ values are [0 0 0], the absolute luminance and relative luminance are identical and it would not matter whether the DCDM were defined in terms of absolute or relative luminance. However, this is never the case. Also, if the theater black were the same in all theaters and at all time, there would be a simple transform from absolute to relative luminance. However, this is never the case. The most common case is that the theater black in a review room has lower XYZ values than the theater black in an exhibition theater. The question then is, "Which luminance encoding, absolute or relative, gives the best overall quality when the same DCDM file is projected in a large number of different theaters?" The answer to this question will determine the best encoding to use in the DCDM.

Consider three theaters with digital projectors that are each calibrated to the white point luminance of 48 cd/m^2. Assume that the first theater has a 2000:1 contrast ratio, which means the theater black luminance is 0.024 cd/m^2, that the second theater is the mastering theater and has a contrast ratio of 2000:1, and that the third theater has a 1000:1 contrast ratio, which means the theater black luminance is 0.048 cd/m^2. Figure 4.12 shows the luminance that would be measured off the screen in both the relative and absolute encoding cases given a series of patches arbitrarily numbered 0, 1, 2, 3, etc.

In Figure 4.12, the heavy black line shows the measured luminance for the first theater and for the mastering theater, the 2000:1 contrast ratio theaters. Because these two theaters have the same contrast ratios, it does not matter if the encoding is absolute or relative; the results are the same for the two theaters. In this example, the third theater, with the 1000:1 contrast ratio, will display two different sets of luminance values for these patches depending on whether absolute or relative luminance encoding is chosen.

If absolute luminance encoding is chosen, the luminance values of these patches will be as shown by the dotted line. The dotted line is hidden by the heavy black line for patches 3 and higher patch numbers, but is a horizontal line for patches 0 to 3. Because it is absolute encoding, the system will display those luminance values it is able to display at the proper luminance values as far into the black as it can go (patches 3 and higher patch numbers) and then the other patches (patches 0 to 3) are all displayed at the 0.048 cd/m^2 luminance. The net result is that although in the 2000:1 contrast ratio theater, patches 0, 1, 2, and 3 were reproduced at different

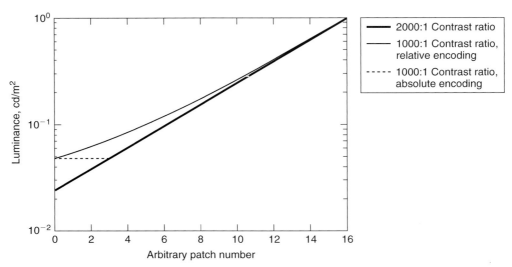

Figure 4-12.   Effect of differing theater contrast ratios on the low luminance levels that can be displayed.

luminance values, in the 1000:1 contrast ratio theater, these patches are all displayed at the same luminance. Therefore these blacks are crushed in the 1000:1 contrast ratio theater.

If relative luminance encoding is chosen, the luminance values of these patches will be as shown by the thin line in Figure 4.12. Both absolute and relative luminance encoding display patches 14 and higher patch numbers as the same (or indistinguishably the same), but the relative encoding displays patches 0 through 13 at higher luminance levels than the absolute encoding displayed the patches. However, the benefit is that all of the patches 0 through 13 are displayed at different luminance values. These patches will appear lighter and lower contrast with the relative encoding than they would appear with the absolute encoding. However, with the relative encoding none of the patches will appear to be crushed. This effect was verified in an experiment using a DLP Cinema® projector, adjusted for different contrast environments. This, then, is the important trade-off between relative and absolute luminance encoding.

If we analyze what is done today with the projection of a film print, we can see that the result is the same as relative encoding. The light reflected from the screen with a projected film print is the sum of the light from the theater black and the light that was modulated by the film print. If the theater black was higher in one theater, the blacks are higher, the contrast in the blacks is lower, but if two black patches have different film densities, they are displayed on the screen at two different luminance values.

There is one other problem that can show up with absolute luminance encoding that does not occur with relative encoding. With relative encoding, because the code values represent levels of light above the minimum light reflected off the screen in the theater, every code value produces some level of light that is projected onto the screen. Therefore, there are no "hidden" or "unseen" code values. But with absolute luminance encoding, every triad of code values defines a color that is supposed to be displayed on the screen. However, if the color is outside the gamut of colors that a particular projector can produce on a screen, for example because the color is darker than the theater black, than that color will be displayed as the theater black because that is the darkest color that can be produced.

So assume an image is being mastered by a system with a particular contrast ratio. With absolute luminance encoding, there will be some code value triads that define a color that cannot be accurately displayed because those colors are darker than the contrast ratio of the system allows. It is possible that some of these code value triads will be placed into the digital file because in the mastering operation, the colors displayed were theater black and that was an acceptable color for that image element. If at some time in the future a system with a larger contrast ratio is used to display this image, the color defined by these code value triads may be displayed properly. Because the encoded color was not seen in mastering, there is the strong possibility that the color produced is not the desired color. Therefore, color errors can occur with absolute luminance encoding if the theater projector has a higher contrast ratio than the mastering projector.

In summary, the difference between absolute encoding and relative encoding shows up when two conditions are met: (1) The mastering projector has a different contrast ratio than a theater projector and (2) There is some content that one projector can accurately display, but the other projector cannot display because it cannot display a black of such low luminance. The use of absolute luminance encoding means the contrast in the black region is maintained to the lowest luminance the lower contrast ratio projector is able to produce, then all darker blacks in the DCDM file are reproduced at the same luminance – hence some blacks are crushed. Conversely, the relative luminance encoding lowers the contrast in the black region, but maintains some differentiation in luminance for all blacks in the DCDM file – hence no blacks are crushed.

Relative encoding was selected for the encoding of the luminance in the DCDM for many reasons. First, the proven film projection system, which is a form of relative encoding, gives good images in theaters with varying theater black levels. Secondly, absolute encoding produces crushed blacks and this loss of detail decreases the quality of an image. And finally, there is the strong possibility that absolute encoding will introduce color errors into the DCDM file if the file is projected with a system with larger contrast ratio than the mastering system. Therefore, the DCDM code values represent the relative luminance above the theater black.

5

Reference Projector and Environment

Since the X'Y'Z' color encoding for digital cinema distribution is an output-referred image state, it is critical that the reference projector that is used for the creative color grading decisions is characterized colorimetrically and calibrated to a common standard. Furthermore, because such imaging parameters as contrast and color gamut constrain what can be displayed, and therefore constrain the creative process, it is necessary to define some minimum performance parameters for the projector to be used in high quality mastering and cinema reproduction. The environment of the mastering room, particularly the ambient light, also influences the quality of the projected image.

These reasons drove DCI and SMPTE DC28 to define the concept of a Reference Projector (and Environment) for Digital Cinema and to define its minimum performance characteristics in a SMPTE Recommended Practice 431.2. This practice was drafted to enable consistent quality in the generation and reproduction of digital cinema masters. The nominal parameters for the Reference Projector are based on current industry practice and have been demonstrated with commercially available projection equipment. Two levels of tolerances are specified, one for critical mastering and screening rooms and another (slightly wider tolerance) for reproduction in cinemas.

Pixel Count

The sampling structure of the displayed picture (pixel count) is defined to be a minimum of 2048 horizontal by 1080 vertical, equivalent to levels 2 or 3 of the DCDM container. This requirement means that a 2K DCDM can be displayed directly, pixel for pixel, without any digital scaling. For 4K mastering (DCDM level 1), a minimum sampling structure of 4096 horizontal by 2160 vertical is desirable for the same reasons. For 4K mastering with a 2K projector, one can work with 2K proxies and display a down-sampled 2K picture, or display a quarter-picture window into the 4K data.

Screen Luminance

Screen Luminance level is a critical parameter, because it impacts the contrast and colorfulness of the projected picture, and therefore has a substantial impact on the creative color grading decisions. In general, a brighter display is capable of producing snappier pictures with higher contrast and a more colorful appearance. However, there are practical limitations to lamp power and operating costs that must be considered when lighting a large cinema screen.

Since the digital cinema transition will not take place overnight, compatibility with the legacy film projectors is an additional requirement. The screen luminance standard for film projection is 16 ft L (open gate), and the digital projector must produce the same peak luminance for the pictures to look the same. It was also the desire of both the studios and the creative community to produce a single master for both film and digital distribution. This means that the creative color grading decisions are made only once. For this condition to apply, it is necessary that the two displays (film and digital projection) be calibrated to a common white point.

A projected film print has a minimum density (D-min) that limits the peak luminance that can be reproduced on the screen. In order to determine the practical peak luminance of a projected film print, DCI collected samples of processed print stock over a period of two weeks from Deluxe and Technicolor, the two major release printing laboratories that provide essentially all of the release printing services for the Hollywood studios. This study showed that the average D-min was 0.07 R, 0.07 G, 0.10 B, resulting in a practical peak luminance of just under 14 ft L, when projected at the 16 ft L open gate standard. This became the basis for the DCI specification for screen luminance and codified in the subsequent SMPTE Standard for Screen Luminance, Chrominance and Uniformity, SMPTE 431.1.

This screen luminance (14 ft L) was used for the DCI-sponsored production of the ASC (American Society of Cinematographers) Standard Evaluation Material (StEM), and proved its merit in a critical side by side comparison with a projected film answer print (see side bar for more information). Previously, the common practice in digital cinema mastering and exhibition had been 12 ft L, and this generally worked well, but the color grading was performed with conventional telecine color correctors, in most cases without highlight compression. It should be noted that a diffuse white card (at approximately 90% reflectance) on film is actually reproduced at about 12 ft L, and that 14 ft L is only practically used for specular highlights and blown-out windows or skies.

White Chromaticity

SMPTE Standard 196M also specifies the open gate chromaticity of white as 0.332 x, 0.347 y, for a correlated color temperature of 5400 degrees K. This is also known as D55. The simple approach would have been to specify the same white point for digital cinema projection. However, current industry practice did not match the standard. This standard was originally based on projectors that used carbon arc lamps, and was adopted for xenon lamps with their introduction in the 1960s. However, with the discontinuance of carbon arc lamps, Xenon lamps and their supporting reflectors were optimized to put more light on bigger screens, and in this process, migrated to a native white point that is much cooler (bluer and greener) than the documented standard.

Digital cinema projectors also use Xenon lamps and in some cases, the same reflectors and lamp houses as traditional film projectors. Maximizing screen luminance is a critical design objective, so digital cinema projectors were designed for a native white point of 0.314 x, 0.351 y (a correlated color temperature of 6300 K). Surveys of installed film projectors have shown that the color temperature varies substantially across the exhibition population. While laboratory screening rooms are typically closer to the 196M standard, this is achieved only by careful selection of reflector materials, with a tradeoff in screen brightness that is not a problem with their smaller screens. The measured white points from a survey of film projectors are shown in Figure 5.1.

Since the human eye adapts fairly well to a wide range of white points, particularly with the display of cinema pictures in a darkened surround, one could argue that a standard white point is not required. In practice, the wide variation in screen white points in exhibition theatres has not created problems, and the audience does not demand their money back. Of course, the general audience doesn't know what the picture is supposed to look like and has no comparison to make a judgment as to whether it is right or wrong. One of the typical complaints of cinematographers and directors who make the creative color decisions in the answer printing process is that the picture rarely looks the same in the cinema. Of course, some of this is due to the analog duplication process described in Chapter 2, much of it to the variation in chemical development of the prints over thousands of film prints, but some of it is also due to the variation in projector white points. Figure 5.2 illustrates the range of white points applied to the StEM midday wedding scene. When compared side by side, these differences are magnified.

So, the general consensus was that specifying a standard white point would lead to more consistent practice, and that the important thing was not the specific white point, but picking one that was practical and efficient to implement. Since the efficient white point for digital cinema projectors (0.314 x, 0.351 y) was also in the center of scatter of survey data from the measured film projectors, this was deemed a reasonable choice.

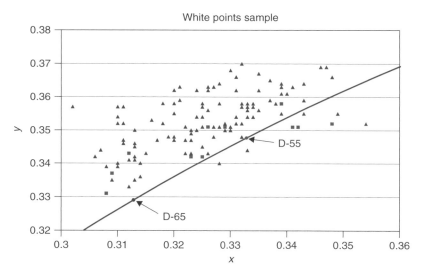

Figure 5-1. Survey of white points of installed film projectors (reported by M. Cowan, 2002). The blue data points were collected by THX in 1999 and 2001. The red data points are based on an earlier report by Glenn Berggren.

Figure 5-2. Comparison of three different white points, with the center image representing the white point chosen for digital cinema [Picture from Standard Evaluation Material (StEM), courtesy of American Society of Cinematographers and Digital Cinema Initiatives].

WHAT REALLY HAPPENS IN CURRENT FILM PROJECTION?

As shown in Figure 5.1, the white point of film projectors varies significantly from one screen to another. However, because the human eye adapts easily to different white points, particularly in a darkened surround with no color reference, this has never been an operational problem.

A bigger issue that does affect the quality of the projected picture is the screen luminance. Although SMPTE 196M calls for a screen luminance of 16 ft L with a minimum tolerance of 11 ft L, in practice the picture is often dimmer than that. The reason is due to both physics and economics—the light output of a Xenon lamp decays over time and lamps are expensive to replace (as much as $2000 for a 5 kW lamp). The typical light output of a Xenon lamp vs. operating time is shown in Figure 5.3.

Some exhibitors minimize their operating costs by running their lamps until they no longer ignite when turned on. This results in a luminance reduction of about 50%, as can be seen from Figure 5.3. This practice has a major impact on the quality of the picture. A print projected at 8 ft L looks dull and dark, lacking contrast, colorfulness and missing important shadow detail. While some digital cinema projectors have built-in compensation that increases the lamp current to maintain the screen brightness as the lamp ages, and many hope that the luminance levels of digital cinema presentation are more carefully controlled so that the audience sees the best picture quality, the underlying economic motivations remain the same with digital as with film.

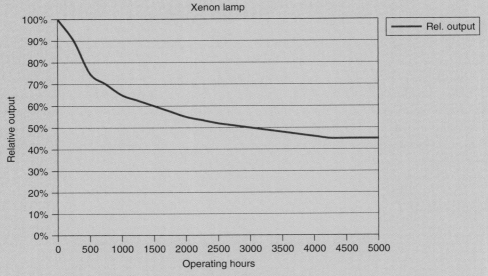

Figure 5-3. Typical light output for a Xenon lamp used in cinema projectors.

Luminance Uniformity

SMPTE 196M also specifies luminance uniformity for film projectors, with luminance of the screen sides (5% in from the picture width) held to 75% to 90% of the screen center value. For review rooms, this specification is tightened to 80% to 90%, and the screen corners are held to this same value. Since it is possible to digitally compensate for luminance shading, some suggested that the digital specification for luminance uniformity should be flat (100%). However, it was pointed out quickly by directors and cinematographers that the typical luminance falloff from center to edges of the screen helps to focus the attention of the audience on the action in screen center, and is therefore a desirable feature. So, the digital cinema specification adopted the same luminance uniformity specifications as film projectors. Just as with film projectors, it was noted that high gain screens often produce less uniform pictures and that screens should be curved to improve uniformity as described in SMPTE RP95.

Color Uniformity

The SMPTE 196M standard does not include a specification for color uniformity of a white field, because this typically was not a problem with film projectors. Some digital projection technologies, on the other hand, suffer from color non-uniformity, so a color uniformity specification was deemed necessary. The theatre specification calls for a white point tolerance of $+/- 0.006$ x and y in the center of the screen, and chrominance uniformity in the corners within $+/- 0.015$ x and y of the center. For review rooms, these specifications are narrowed to $+/- 0.002$ x and y for the center, and $+/- 0.008$ x and y for the corners relative to the center.

These parameters, along with others that will be described shortly, are summarized in Table 5-A. This table includes the nominal parameters for the Reference Projector, as well as tolerances for mastering/review rooms and for exhibition theatres. It is important to note that all of these parameters are measured off the screen and include the contribution of any ambient light in the room. The nominal parameters for the Reference Projector are based on industry experience and have been measured from commercially available projectors. So that future improvements in projection technology are not precluded, some of these parameters are specified as minimum values rather than tolerances.

Sequential Contrast

The sequential contrast ratio is computed by dividing the luminance of the peak white by the luminance of black (code value zero). This is a very important image quality parameter for digital cinema and an area where recent improvements in sequential contrast to 2000:1 (from 1200:1) have gone a long way towards closing the gap between film and digital projection. Although a

Sec.	Image Parameters	Nominal (Reference Projector)	Tolerances (Review Rooms)	Tolerances (Theatres)
7.1	Pixel Count	2048*1080 or greater	2048*1080 or greater	2048*1080 or greater
7.2	Luminance Uniformity, corners and sides	85% of center	80% to 90% of center	70% to 90% of center
7.3	Calibrated White Luminance, center	48 cd/m^2 (14 fL)	±2.4 cd/m^2 (±0.7 fL)	±10.2 cd/m^2 (±3.0 fL)
7.3	Calibrated White Chromaticity, center from code values [3794 3960 3890]	x = .314, y = .351	±.002 x, y	±.006 x, y
7.4	Color Uniformity of White Field, corners	matches center	±.008 x, y Relative to center	±.015 x, y Relative to center
7.5	Sequential Contrast	2000:1 minimum	1500:1 minimum	1200:1 minimum
7.6	Intra-frame Contrast	150:1 minimum	100:1 minimum	100:1 minimum
7.7	Grayscale Tracking	No visible color shading	No visible color shading	No visible color shading
7.8	Contouring	Continuous, smooth ramp, with no visible steps	(same)	(same)
7.9	Transfer Function	Gamma 2.6	±2%[1]	±5% Best fit
7.10	Color Gamut	Minimum Color Gamut enclosed by white point, black point[2] and Red: 0.680 x, 0.320 y, 10.1 Y Green: 0.265 x, 0.690 y, 34.6 Y Blue: 0.150 x, 0.060 y, 3.3 Y	(same)	(same)
7.11	Color Accuracy	Colorimetric Match	4 delta E*	4 delta E*

1. Least squares fit of slope of log/log plot of measured luminance vs. input code value, using a range from peak white luminance down to 5% of peak white.
2. The luminance of the black point is limited by the sequential contrast ratio of the projector plus the ambient light falling on the screen.

Table 5-A. Reference Projector Image Parameters and Tolerances for Review Rooms and Theatres
The Reference Projector image parameters and tolerances for the projected image in Review Rooms and Exhibition Theatres, as measured off the screen and including the room ambient light, are summarized here.

film print is capable of a density range of over 4.0 (10,000:1) this immense range is limited by the dynamic range of the negative and further reduced by projection flare, so that the sequential contrast range of typical projected print is only about 3000:1. With sequential contrast, a bigger number is always better, so this is specified as a minimum sequential contrast of 1500:1 for mastering and review rooms and 1200:1 for cinemas.

Figure 5-4.   Checkerboard target for ANSI (in-frame) contrast measurements.

Intra-frame Contrast

There is another important contrast parameter that affects the quality of a projected image. This is the contrast within a single frame, or the intra-frame contrast. Typically this is measured with a checkerboard target per ANSI specifications, and is often referred to as Checkerboard contrast or ANSI contrast. This target is shown in Figure 5.4. This parameter depends not only on the performance of the image modulator, but is also affected by the projection lens flare, the portal glass, back-reflections off of walls and seating and even dust in the atmosphere.

Manufacturers typically measure the ANSI contrast of their projectors using an incident light meter pointed at the lens with the projector set up in a black non-reflective room to minimize reflections and flare. This type of measurement method produces intra-frame contrast numbers of over 500:1 for typical DLP Cinema® projectors, but these numbers are not representative of real world performance given the other factors mentioned above.

When the same projectors are measured with a reflective light meter pointed at a typical theatre screen, a typical intra-frame contrast number is less than 200:1. If the same checkerboard target is recorded onto film, printed and measured from the image of the projected print on the screen, a typical intra-frame contrast measurement for a film projector with a standard projection lens is only about 150:1. Considering these benchmarks, the nominal value for intra-frame contrast was established at 150:1 minimum, with the tolerance for review rooms and exhibition theatres set at 100:1 minimum.

Transfer Function

The transfer function of a digital cinema projector is specified by a power law of gamma 2.6, as was described in Chapter 4. The specified tolerance for this gamma is +/− 2% for review rooms and +/− 5% for exhibition theatres. The gamma is measured as a least squares fit of the slope of

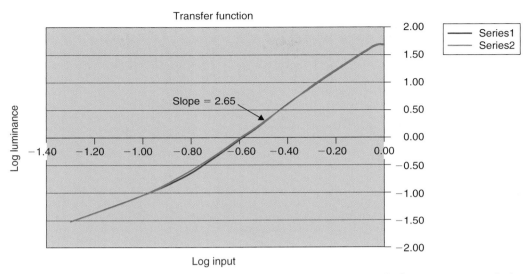

Figure 5-5. Gamma is computed by measuring the slope of a log-log plot of the transfer function, comparing the log of the measured screen luminances to the log of the input signal. This data was measured from two DLP Cinema projectors.

a log/log plot of measured luminance vs. input code value, using a range from peak white luminance down to 5% of peak white. An example of transfer function and gamma measurement from a typical DLP Cinema® projector is shown in Figure 5.5.

Color Gamut

As was noted before, the DLP Cinema® color gamut was extended from its initial ITU-R Rec. 709 gamut to a wider gamut that approximates that of a projected film print. This wider color gamut has been used successfully for over 150 digital releases, and was judged to be an acceptable starting point for the color gamut of the Reference Projector for digital cinema.

The gamut of reproducible colors in an additive color system is a parallelepiped (six-sided solid with five vertices). The vertices are defined by the white point, black point and the three color primaries. Note that all luminance information falls on a straight line of constant chromaticity between the white and black points. The color gamut of the Reference Projector is illustrated in Figure 5.6, with the chromaticity and luminance coordinates of each vertex shown in Table 5-B. It is important to note that this color gamut is specified as the minimum color gamut for digital cinema mastering and exhibition, and that technology improvements in wider gamut illumination sources (such as lasers) may someday allow for wider gamut display.

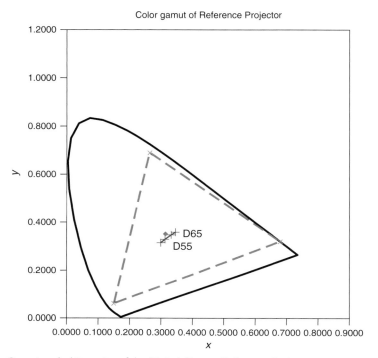

Figure 5-6. Color Gamut and white point of the Digital Cinema Reference Projector.

	x	y
Red	0.680	0.320
Green	0.265	0.690
Blue	0.150	0.060
White	0.314	0.351

Table 5-B. Color primaries and white point of the Digital Cinema Reference Projector.

Color Accuracy

Within this minimum color gamut, all colors should also be accurately reproduced. SMPTE RP 431.2 specifies a colorimetric tolerance of +/− 4 delta E_{ab}^* units, where E_{ab}^* represents the magnitude of the color error vector in a*, b* uniform color coordinates.

Environment

The room environment plays a critical role in the quality of the projected image, because any stray light that falls on the screen reduces the contrast of the projected image. It is critically important that special measures be taken to minimize stray light in the design of the room, and the placement of working and safety lights. This is more easily done with mastering rooms or critical screening rooms, because building codes and municipal safety requirements for commercial cinemas dictate floor lights for safe egress and lighted exit signs above the doors. Unfortunately, the design of the room often means that some of this light falls on the screen.

For mastering and screening rooms where critical color correction and approval decisions are made, however, several simple rules can be followed to insure that stray light is minimized and that the projected image is viewed in the highest quality environment.

Matte black, non-reflecting surfaces should be used wherever possible. This means black carpet, black seating, black walls, and a black ceiling. Dark gray and muted dark accent colors are acceptable and go a long way to appeasing the interior designer without impairing the picture on the screen. Reflective surfaces should be avoided, because the projected picture will be reflected from the screen back into the room and back-reflected from any bright or shiny surface. Even white clothing will do this—it's a good thing that the creative folks like to wear black!

Exit doors should not be placed next to the screen, but should be placed in the back of the room and recessed so that light from the signs doesn't spill onto the screen. Floor lights for guiding entrance and exiting should be small and low power (perhaps LED) and located under the arms of the end chairs, directed at the floor, not up at the screen. Likewise, working lights on color correction consoles or client desks should be placed carefully, directed down narrowly on the work surface and dimmable from the colorist's console.

The SMPTE RP Reference Projector specifies that the ambient light level reflected from the screen shall be less than 0.01 cd/m^2 (0.0029 ft L). This is measured with the projector lamp turned off or douser closed on the projector. Frankly, this light level is too low to be measured with commonly available instrumentation (more on that later). Keep in mind that the luminance of peak white is 48 cd/m^2 (14 ft L), so this level of ambient light supports a sequential contrast of up to 4800:1, more than twice as good as projectors currently used in mastering. But one can see the difference between 2000:1 and 4000:1 and film prints are capable of a sequential contrast of over 4000:1. Furthermore, digital cinema projectors are expected to offer improved contrast in the not so distant future, so the room design and its ambient lighting should not be the limiting factor.

The screen surface is specified to be Lambertian, which means that it reflects spectral energy uniformly across all viewing angles, such that the color of the reflected light does not change with the viewing angle. In mastering and screening rooms, a flat matte (1.0 gain) screen is recommended for uniformity. If the design of the room requires the placement of speakers behind the screen, it may be necessary to use perforations; however, care should be taken to insure that the perforation structure does not beat against (alias with) the display structure of the projected image. In mastering rooms used for critical color grading, a non-perforated screen is strongly recommended. For small review rooms used for quality control or final approvals with sound, micro-perforations are recommended.

The screen should be equipped with adjustable black masking, which can be moved to tightly frame the projected image, for each of 1.85:1 and 2.39:1 projected image formats. A tight, clean black border is critical to the quality of the projected picture. You do not want to put a 2.39:1 picture on a 1.85:1 screen, without masking the top and bottom. Otherwise the large white border impairs the contrast of the projected image.

The reference viewing position for color grading and quality control decisions should be at a viewing distance of 1.5 to 3.5 screen heights, with 2.0 screen heights generally accepted as the optimum position. At 2.0 screen heights, a person with 20:20 corrected vision can see all the fine detail in the picture, but yet is far enough back to see the whole picture without moving his or her head from side to side.

Calibration

The projector shall be calibrated to the white point and primaries of the Reference Projector once it is installed in its working environment. This will compensate for any slight discolorations introduced by the screen or portal glass. This is not to say that low quality materials can be used for either screens or portal glass. Only clean, uniform professional screens and angled portals employing optical glass with anti-reflection coatings should be used. The interior pane of a dual-pane portal is angled so that any back-reflected light is deflected outside of the lens to minimize flare.

This calibration process is simply a matter of measuring the chromaticities of the primaries and white, using internally generated (or externally supplied) red, green, blue and white field test patterns. A calibrated spectro-radiometer is used for these measurements. Following the manufacturer's instructions, the projector is then calibrated such that the measured chromaticities are dialed in to match those of the standard Reference Projector.

> ### AUTOMATED CALIBRATION OF DLP CINEMA® PROJECTORS
>
> For DLP Cinema® projectors, the measured chromaticities are entered into the Measured Color Gamut Data (MCGD) file through the projector's service menu. The operator selects the standard Target Color Gamut Data (TCGD) file, which includes the chromaticity parameters of the primaries and white point of the Reference Projector, and the projector automatically computes a linear space 3×3 matrix to convert from the measured color gamut to the target color gamut. This color space conversion is based on the same principles that will be described in Chapter 7 and 8.

Instrumentation

A spot photometer is used to measure screen luminance, with a spectral response of the CIE standard observer (photopic vision), as defined in CIE S002. The photometer should have a collection angle of 2 degrees or less. For white field measurements, an accuracy of ± 0.5 cd/m^2 (± 0.2 fL) is required. For black field measurements, an accuracy of ± 0.007 cd/m^2 (± 0.002 fL) is specified. In order to provide stable readings that are insensitive to flicker, the photometer must integrate over a period of time sufficient to remove all frequencies above 24 Hz, displaying the arithmetic mean value. The Konica Minolta LS-110 is a commonly used photometer in the motion picture industry.

Chromaticity measurements should be made with a spot spectro-radiometer, that provides outputs in CIE x, y, Y coordinates. An acceptance angle of 2 degrees or less shall be used for these measurements. An accuracy of ± 0.002 or better for both x and y at luminance above 10 cd/m^2 is required. The Photo Research PR-650 and Konica Minolta CS-1000 are commonly used spectrophotometers that meet these requirements.

Measurement Locations

For mastering rooms, the measurement location shall be at the colorist's working position in the room, with the instrument placed on a tripod at eye level. In small screening rooms, the measurement location shall be from the "Director's seat" in the center of the seating area.

For exhibition theatres, the SMPTE RP 431.3 on Digital Cinema Projection Image Measurements specifies six measurement locations: three in the center row of the theatre and three in the rear row of the theatre. The three locations within each row are the far left seat, the center seat and the far right seat. At each measurement location, the instrument is placed at the eye level of the seated cinema patron, with an average height of 1.1 meters above the floor. Although projector calibration is performed using the data from the "best seat" in the house, the center seat of the center row of the auditorium, the other data is collected to build a profile of how performance varies with viewing angle. Screen Luminance and uniformity, for example, can vary substantially form center to edge in a large auditorium with a high gain screen.

Test Patterns

A variety of test patterns are used to measure the performance of a projector. These include the full-field white, red, green and blue frames that are used for calibration and white field uniformity measurements, plus a black field that is used along with the white field for the measurement of sequential contrast. Intra-frame contrast is measured with a checkerboard pattern of 16 patches, alternating white and black. These test patterns are shown in Figure 5.7, with annotations indicating the X'Y'Z' digital code values of each patch.

Table 5-C from the SMPTE RP on Reference Projector provides a set of color patches for verifying the color accuracy of a calibrated projector. Two levels of color saturation are provided; one at the minimum gamut specified for the Reference Projector and a second set that is pulled in such that it fits with the color gamut of ITU Rec. 709.

The SMPTE RP 431.2 on Reference Projector and Environment also includes two tables that define 10-step grayscale values for evaluation of grayscale tracking. There are two grayscales, one that covers the full range from black to white, and another that covers a smaller range from black to dark gray. These two tables are reproduced below.

A grid test pattern is also very useful for evaluating size, geometry, convergence and focus. Circles are often added to grid patterns to evaluate geometry, because the human observer is particularly sensitive to geometric distortions that affect the uniform roundness of a circle. An example of a typical grid pattern (with circles) is included in Figure 5.8.

Contouring is the appearance of steps or bands where only a continuous or smooth gradient should be seen. Because contouring is a function of many variables, it is important to look at a series of test patterns with shallow gradations to simulate naturally occurring gradations in images. Naturally occurring examples include horizons, particularly at sunset or sunrise, and the natural falloff around high intensity spotlights, particularly if diffused by atmosphere or lens filtration. These test pattern ramps should have a step width of no less than 4 pixels with an increment of one code value per step and should be placed on a background equal to the minimum value in the ramp, so that the eye is adapted for maximum sensitivity. Since dynamic fades to black are widely used in real-world content, a dynamic test pattern that fades slowly to black is another useful approach.

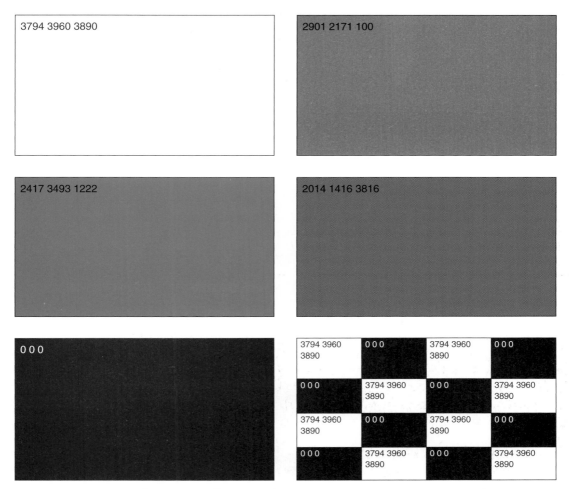

Figure 5-7. Test patterns for projector calibration and measurement.

Each image shall be viewed under normal viewing distance and operating condition, and should not exhibit any contouring (step in luminance), or color deviation from the neutral gray.

Measurements

The ambient light in the room is measured off the center of the screen with operational safety lights and working lights turned on, but with the projector lamp doused or turned off. Ambient light is the room light that is not created by the projector.

Patch	Input Code Values[*]			Output Chromaticity Coordinates		Output Luminance
	X'	Y'	Z'	x	y	Y, cd/m²
Red-1	2901	2171	100	0.6800	0.3200	10.06
Green-1	2417	3493	1222	0.2650	0.6900	34.64
Blue-1	2014	1416	3816	0.1500	0.0600	3.31
Cyan-1	2911	3618	3890	0.2048	0.3602	37.94
Magenta-1	3289	2421	3814	0.3424	0.1544	13.36
Yellow-1	3494	3853	1221	0.4248	0.5476	44.69
Red-2	2738	2171	1233	0.5980	0.3269	10.06
Green-2	2767	3493	2325	0.2884	0.5282	34.64
Blue-2	1800	1416	3203	0.1664	0.0891	3.31
Cyan-2	3085	3590	3756	0.2409	0.3572	37.19
Magenta-2	3062	2421	3497	0.3382	0.1838	13.36
Yellow-2	3461	3777	2065	0.3973	0.4989	42.46

Note: Patches labelled -1 and -2 represent two levels of color saturation within the minimum color gamut of the Reference Projector, with the saturation of level-2 reduced so that it falls within the smaller ITU Rec. 709 color gamut.

Table 5-C. Test patches for measuring color accuracy, with corresponding code values, luminance values, and chromaticity coordinates. All measurements shall be made in the center of the screen.

Step Number	Input Code Values[*]			Output Chromaticity Coordinates		Output Luminance[1]
	X'	Y'	Z'	x	y	Y, cd/m²
1	379	396	389	0.314	0.351	0.14
2	759	792	778	0.314	0.351	0.75
3	1138	1188	1167	0.314	0.351	2.12
4	1518	1584	1556	0.314	0.351	4.45
5	1897	1980	1945	0.314	0.351	7.94
6	2276	2376	2334	0.314	0.351	12.74
7	2656	2772	2723	0.314	0.351	19.01
8	3035	3168	3112	0.314	0.351	26.89
9	3415	3564	3501	0.314	0.351	36.52
10	3794	3960	3890	0.314	0.351	48.00

1. Output luminance includes 0.024 cd/m² screen black level (representing a 2000:1 contrast ratio).

Table 5-D. Black-to-white gray step-scale test pattern code values, luminance values, and chromaticity coordinates (all measurements are made in the center of the screen).

Step Number	Input Code Values*			Output Chromaticity Coordinates		Output Luminance[2]
	X'	Y'	Z'	x	y	Y, cd/m²
1	122	128	125	0.314	0.351	0.030
2	245	255	251	0.314	0.351	0.063
3	367	383	376	0.314	0.351	0.135
4	490	511	502	0.314	0.351	0.254
5	612	639	627	0.314	0.351	0.442
6	734	766	753	0.314	0.351	0.695
7	857	894	878	0.314	0.351	1.026
8	979	1022	1004	0.314	0.351	1.442
9	1101	1150	1129	0.314	0.351	1.950
10	1224	1277	1255	0.314	0.351	2.557
2. Ditto.						

Table 5-E. Black-to-dark gray step-scale test pattern code values, luminance values, and chromaticity coordinates (all measurements are made in the center of the screen).

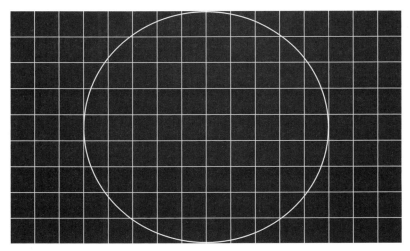

Figure 5-8. Grid pattern for evaluating projector geometry, convergence and focus.

The picture is focused with the grid test pattern, adjusting the lens focus ring so that individual pixels can be detected when viewing the projected image within one meter of the screen. If the screen is perforated, it may be necessary to place a white card against the screen so that the perforations don't hide the pixels of the projected image.

The full-field white test frame is used to measure luminance level and chromaticity of white (from the center of the screen) It is also used to measure luminance uniformity and color uniformity of white, dividing the screen into 3 × 3 blocks and comparing the four sides and four corners of screen to the luminance and chromaticity of the center. It may be necessary to realign the reflectors in the lamp house if the projector does not meet the luminance or chrominance uniformity specified by SMPTE Standard 431.1 D-Cinema Screen Luminance Level, Chromaticity and Uniformity.

Sequential contrast is measured from the ratio of the luminance of the white field divided by that of the black field (measured from the center of the screen). It is important to note that this is the sequential contrast of the projector in its operating environment. Ambient light reduces the sequential contrast of the projector itself.

Intra-frame (or ANSI contrast) is measured with the Checkerboard target shown earlier in Figure 5.3. The luminance of each of the white patches and each of the black patches is measured with a spot photometer. Intra-frame contrast is then computed by summing the white patches and dividing by the sum of the black patches. In its operating environment, the intra-frame contrast is reduced by many factors including projection lens flare, portal glass flare, ambient light spilling onto the screen and back reflections from the room itself.

Requirements for the Mastering Projector

Because the mastering projector is the reference for the creative color decisions and is used for the quality control of the picture, it is critical that the mastering projector be calibrated to the Reference Projector specification. It is also important that the mastering projector represent the "best in class" in terms of contrast, color gamut and sharpness, otherwise unwanted details or artifacts may be invisible in the mastering room, but could show up down the line in exhibition. So, as projection technology evolves, it is incumbent on the post production facilities and their clients to insure that they are using "best in class" projectors.

6
Digital Mastering

Before we consider the color encoding for digital cinema distribution, it is useful to take a step back and look at the creative process as it applies to feature film post production. This process has evolved from the traditional film process described in Chapter 2 and has embraced digital technologies over the last fifteen or so years.

The first step in the filmmaking process to embrace digital technology was editing. Traditionally this process was performed manually by cutting and splicing film prints on an upright Moviola or flatbed KEM editing system. These systems were essentially miniature projectors with film transports that could be rolled forward or reverse or paused on a single frame. But this process was very labor intensive, linear and slow. In the 1980s, George Lucas invested in the development of the EditDroid™, the first computer-based non-linear digital image editing system (with pictures stored on laserdisc). Although this system was not broadly commercialized, it did show the value of computer based editing, and encouraged several other companies to develop products. By the end of the 1990's, the Avid Media Composer was the ubiquitous off-line non-linear editing system for film and video post production. Today, essentially all feature films are edited with digital non-linear editing systems, and this technology, along with the creative vision of directors schooled in short-form music video and commercials production, has led to a much faster paced, rapid-cutting style in many action films.

Visual Effects (VFX) was the second step in the filmmaking process to embrace digital technology in post production. The development of CCD film scanners and CRT film recorders in the late 1980's, foretold the rapid demise of the optical printer. With the opening of Kodak's Cinesite Digital Film Center in 1992, high quality, cost-effective digital film scanning and recording services were made available to everyone. The introduction of the Kodak Cineon Digital Film Compositing software and Discreet Logic's Flame and Inferno in the mid 90's led the way with creative tools for building visual effects. Many of the larger visual effects facilities like ILM, Sony Imageworks and Digital Domain also developed their own software tools. By the end of the 1990's, desktop software packages from companies like Adobe and Apple were also in widespread use.

Although Kodak and many others in the industry had foreseen the use of digital technology for the assembly and grading of full feature films, the technology was not fast or inexpensive enough to make this practical in 1992. In fact, it took nearly a decade for full feature films to be posted digitally. When Kodak established a Digital Mastering department at Cinesite in 1998, it coined the term "Digital Intermediate" to refer to the application of digital conforming, image processing and color grading to full feature films, and the generation of a digital inter-negative for traditional release printing. Since this process was conceived as an intermediate post production step between film acquisition and film distribution, and since it generated a new "digital inter-negative", the term "Digital Intermediate" took hold.

Most people agree that the first full live-action film to be digitally conformed and color graded was "Pleasantville", in 1998. Since this movie involved a unique technique for eliminating color and gradually and selectively bringing it back through rotoscoping, it was really a large-scale visual effects project. However, it represents the first Hollywood film to use digital tools for conforming and grading a full feature film, with the final master recorded back to a film inter-negative for release printing. A Philips Spirit Datacine was used with a DaVinci color corrector to provide a graded scan. The rest of the process, including rotoscoping, conforming and final grading was performed using customized software. At the same time as Cinesite was pioneering this process in Hollywood, others in Europe were applying a similar process to European feature films. Duboi, in France, and Digital Film Lab in Copenhagen, were early pioneers.

At the beginning of 2000, Cinesite embarked on an ambitious digital intermediate project with the Coen Brothers' "O Brother, Where art Thou?", a film shot by Roger Deakins in the lush green fields of Mississippi. However, the Coen Brothers wanted to make this film look like it was shot in a dry and dusty environment, as well as making it look in parts like an old sepia photograph, turning the green to a mustard yellow, while preserving skin tones and other colors important to the story. This could not be achieved with camera filters or conventional sepia tone printing, and Roger Deakins realized that a digital intermediate was required. Furthermore, since he wanted to shoot with standard (non-anamorphic) camera lenses, but frame for wide-screen (2.39) release, the Super-35 process was required. The digital intermediate process provided a key advantage here—the digital conversion from full aperture (flat) 35 mm to anamorphic 35 mm for release is a much cleaner and sharper conversion than a traditional optical blowup.

The select shots from the original camera negative were scanned (with handles) at 2K resolution on a Spirit Datacine, and graded by Colorist Julius Friede using a Pandora MegaDef color corrector with output to DPX data files for film recording. Since the available digital projection technology at the time did not support the contrast range required for the film print output, a CRT monitor was used for grading reference, supplemented by a custom display 1-D lookup table to apply the print film's characteristic "S"-curve. The capability to use 3-D color lookup tables for display was not yet available. It soon became clear that the 1-D color tables did not accurately represent the saturated yellows of the print film, so the color correction decisions made in post production were not delivered faithfully to the film output. Because of this, extra color correction passes were required to dial in the desired result. The total process, including digital opticals, integration of VFX shots and output to film took about three months.

Fortunately, the technology, software tools and infrastructure have all come a long way since "O Brother", with 3-D LUTs for more accurate film emulation with state-of-the-art DLP Cinema® projectors, software tools for conforming and color correction, and faster film recording. Let's fast forward to 2006. Deluxe/E-Film and Technicolor have both have built substantial infrastructure to routinely finish digital intermediate projects in 4–6 weeks, and these two facilities combined to deliver over 50 projects in 2005 alone. At least ten other post production facilities had built and offered digital intermediate services by the end of 2005, with more than thirty mastering suites equipped with DLP Cinema® projectors. This provides enough capacity to support all of the major studio releases in Hollywood, and most studio post production executives predict that nearly all of their movies will be finished digitally, if not by the end of 2006, at least by some time in the following year.

Color grading for film and digital cinema release is accomplished in a mastering room equipped with a 20–30 ft wide screen and a digital cinema projector. Figure 6.1 shows a DI mastering theatre at Laser Pacific.

With large scale deployment of digital cinema systems beginning in 2006, it is indeed fortunate timing that the post production community has invested in enough capacity to support a digital intermediate process that provides a digital finish for both film and digital cinema release. The same digital master that is output to film to create an inter-negative for film release printing can easily be converted into the Digital Cinema Distribution Master (DCDM). For most digital intermediate processes, it is simply a matter of rendering or "baking in" the print film characteristic in the form of the 3D LUT that is used in the reference display.

The digital intermediate process is very different from the traditional home video mastering process whereby a color-timed film Interpositive (IP) is transferred to a videotape master and color corrected on a scene to scene basis using a hardware color corrector, using a timed work print as a reference. In terms of workflow, the digital intermediate process more closely resembles episodic television.

Figure 6-1.   Digital Intermediate Color Grading Theatre at Laser Pacific Media Corporation.

Digital, computer-based architectures break the linear, real-time paradigm that characterized the traditional home video mastering process. With distributed computer architectures and resolution-independent software, it is possible to parallel many activities, compiling the instructions and then rendering the final result. Resolution and color space conversions can also be automated to create the necessary outputs to support various distribution formats.

Although processes vary from facility to facility, they tend to be based on networked storage that is shared between multiple applications running on general purpose computers. Because of the bandwidth requirements of interactive color grading and real-time playback, hardware accelerators and high performance disk systems and output cards are incorporated in many workstations.

Figure 6.2 shows the architecture of a typical digital intermediate process. This diagram is grouped into three sections—inputs, digital intermediate data, and outputs. In addition to film prints and the digital cinema distribution master, the output section also includes the various HD and SD home video masters. Although film is the primary input source today, digital origination is shown as an alternative input path. This workflow has centralized data storage connected via high speed networking.

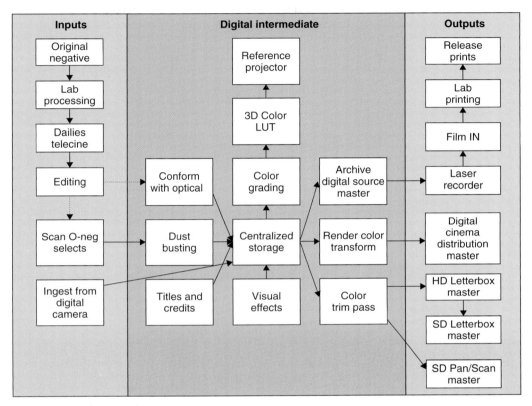

Figure 6-2. Digital Intermediate Process.

For film origination, the first step is to process the original negative at the film laboratory, then transfer the select scenes to video for digital dailies and off-line editing. The output of the process is compressed video files for an Avid or other off-line editing system, and HD videotape, DVD or compressed video files for dailies. If digital cameras are being used, then this process is reduced to an ingestion and compression operation (the film processing and telecine transfer at the lab are eliminated).

Once the movie is edited, or at least a rough cut has been assembled, a negative pull list is generated from the edit decision list. This is used to pull the original negative rolls based on their key-codes. These rolls are scanned with handles (extra frames) on a Datacine™ or pin-registered film scanner that is calibrated to deliver the full range of the original negative film. The data is typically stored in 10-bit log (printing density) format within DPX or Cineon files. The shots are conformed to the final EDL, including the generation of fades, dissolves or other "optical" transitions between shots. Finished visual effects shots are imported and inserted for color grading in continuity.

The next step is color grading the assembled shots in a mastering suite equipped with a calibrated DLP Cinema® projector. Most processes use a display 3-D Color LUT to emulate a film print, with this LUT implemented either in the color corrector, an external LUT box, or inside the projector. This LUT is tuned for the characteristics of the specific print stock and lab that will be used for release printing. This is a film-centric approach, based on film origination and with distribution on print film as the primary output. An alternative (digital-centric) approach will be discussed later in this chapter.

Color grading is more than just adjusting or correcting the color from scene to scene to provide consistency and continuity. It also helps to impart the emotional context of the story, and complements the lighting and exposure used by the cinematographer to capture the scene. Color correctors provide a range of controls, generally grouped into primary, secondary and windows. The primary color correction controls adjust parameters that were originally implemented inside the telecine—these control the gain (white), gamma (midscale) and lift (black) in each of the red, green and blue records. The secondary controls mix the color primaries to create color difference signals that allow individual hues to be selected and rotated, with this processing originally occurring in a secondary hardware processor.

Figure 6-3.   Control panel and monitoring displays used for digital color grading with the Autodesk Lustre color corrector.

Although the initial color correctors were analog processors, digital technology was incorporated in the 1980's, allowing much more control and flexibility with higher quality. One of the digitally enabled features was the introduction of "Power Windows" that allowed the colorist to draw mattes that applied selective color correction to the windowed region of the frame. These mattes can be tracked and animated as the subject or camera moves. Soft-edged mattes make the edges invisible. This powerful capability allows the cinematographer to digitally "dodge and burn" shots, adding or subtracting light to enhance the original photography. This can be used to fix mistakes, but more frequently is used to save time in production, reducing the need for re-lighting or waiting for just the right natural light.

Operations like removing dirt, commonly called "dustbusting" and title and credit generation are performed in parallel on separate workstations. Conforming, including opticals, can also continue in parallel. The fully assembled master is previewed with the director and/or editor for final approval before rendering the color grading, opticals, dirt fixes and titles into the finished digital master.

The finished digital master, called the Digital Source Master (DSM) in the DCI specification and some SMPTE digital cinema documents, is sent to a bank of film recorders for output to one or more inter-negatives for release printing. The widely used ArriLaser™ film recorder runs at about 2 seconds per frame, so a typical 20 minute reel requires 16 hours of continuous recording.

As described in Chapter 2, each inter-negative can produce from 1000 to 2000 release prints on a high speed release printer before accumulating dirt or scratches that make it unsuitable for further printing. Therefore, a wide release (3000–5000 prints or more) will require multiple inter-negatives. This can be accommodated by using the conventional IP/IN photochemical duplicating process, but this introduces another two generations of losses. The preferred approach is to generate multiple inter-negatives so that each release print is made directly from the digitally-recorded inter-negative, so that each print is essentially a "digital show print".

The only other way to address this bottleneck at film recording is to approve the movie one reel at a time, and output each reel as it is finished. This allows the project to be delivered reel by reel, much as in the traditional answer printing process. However, this means that the director or cinematographer must lock his decisions one reel at a time, and forego one of the big advantages of the digital intermediate process—the flexibility to keep adjusting and improving the movie up until the deadline for sending it to the lab.

Since the movie was graded on a projector that is calibrated to the DCI/SMPTE Reference Projector specifications, the creative work on the Digital Cinema Distribution Master is done. All that remains is to render the 3D color LUT that was used in the grading process into the digital master, along with a simple color conversion to X'Y'Z' (to be described in the next chapter). This can be implemented as a software batch process, or if working in 2K, it can be a real-time output through an external 3D LUT box.

It is also possible to combine this color rendering and color conversion process with the JPEG2000 compression and encryption processing necessary to generate the picture track file for packaging with the sound tracks and subtitles for digital cinema distribution. If working in 2K, then this whole process can be accomplished as a real-time lay down.

The next step is to generate the video masters for DVD and television distribution. Traditionally, home video masters were generated by transferring a color-timed IP on a telecine, with a colorist grading each scene on a calibrated video reference monitor. This process often took an additional 2 to 4 weeks and required supervision of the cinematographer or director, whose time is often difficult to schedule with other competing projects. With digital intermediate, much of the work of creating the various video masters can be automated, and that which requires supervision and approval can be accomplished quickly in a couple of days while the files are still on line and the cinematographer is still available.

Conversion to video for output requires two important processes. The first is framing and composition for video, which involves a panning operation to extract the appropriate part of the widescreen frame for the full-frame 4:3 standard definition video outputs. This process is called "pan/scan" because it traditionally was implemented at the telecine stage and required a second scanning pass to lay down the full frame version. With digital intermediate, this means overlaying a 4:3 framing rectangle and moving it as necessary to capture the most important part of the action.

The second process is to correct the color and tone scale of the picture for the very different characteristics and viewing conditions of a home video display. Remember that the movie was color graded on a digital cinema projector in a dark theatre. The home video display has traditionally been a fairly small CRT television set, viewed in a living room. This viewing environment typically includes some room light which fills in the shadows and increases the perceived contrast of the image. SMPTE RP166 defines a Recommended Practice for Critical Viewing Conditions for the Evaluation of Color Television Pictures that prescribes a dim surround that is 10% of the peak luminance of the monitor and matches the D65 color temperature of the monitor.

But grading for video is more than just a tone scale correction for surround illumination that could be implemented with a simple color transform. The gamut of the HD video display (ITU-R Recommendation 709) is much smaller than that of print film or the Reference Display for digital cinema. So, it is necessary to map some colors that fall within the displayed color gamut of reference projector, but are outside of the color gamut of the video monitor. Although this could be implemented in a global 3D LUT that compressed out of gamut colors, this compression must be implemented as a soft-clip or gradual ramp that also affects some of the in-gamut colors. So, it is always best to look at each scene and selectively apply the gamut mapping only when required. For these reasons, a color trim pass is often used to generate the video masters. However, this trim pass can typically be performed in a day or two, rather than the 2 to 4 weeks of the traditional mastering process.

2K or 4K

One of the most hotly contested debates within the studio technical community has been the question of what resolution to use for digital mastering and distribution. The studios are evenly divided between two opinions—2K (2048 pixels wide) is good enough and much more cost effective, or, let's not set the bar too low; go with 4K (4096 pixels wide) to raise the bar. This debate raged for nearly a year, before DCI arrived at the grand compromise of supporting both 2K and 4K digital cinema distribution masters, using the hierarchical structure of JPEG2000 compression to provide a compatible delivery vehicle.

Working in 4K requires four times the storage and four times the rendering time as 2K. However, it does not cost four times as much. The input scanning and output film recording processes take roughly twice as long. The creative color grading process for 4K can be done in essentially the same time as 2K, so long as the images are sub-sampled to 2K proxies to support inter-active adjustment and display. These color corrections can be stored and rendered to the 4K images once the reel has been approved. Several of the software-based color correctors support this architecture, including products from Autodesk, Filmlight, Nucoda, and DaVinci. If you consider all of these operations in aggregate, there is a significant extra cost of working in 4K rather than 2K today, but the difference is expected to lessen over time.

So what do you get for working in 4K? Does it produce pictures that are twice as good? If the original film format is 35 mm (the overwhelmingly popular choice), and the release format is 35 mm (the only viable film distribution format except for 70 mm IMAX), then the answer is no. The difference between 2K and 4K is much more subtle, and very dependent on the quality of the camera lenses. In a seminal paper by Brad Hunt of Kodak in the March 1991 SMPTE Journal, he described the basis for Kodak's development of a 4K High Resolution Electronic Intermediate System in 1992 (which became Cineon), using a system MTF analysis to illustrate the effect of sampling resolution on the resulting images[1]. This is reproduced in Figure 6.4.

Kodak modeled the system modulation transfer function (MTF) as a function of sampling resolution in order to define the resolution requirements for its film scanners and recorders. Figure Y shows the system MTF responses for a sampling series of 1000 to 5000 samples per picture width

1. B. Hunt, et al., "High Resolution Electronic Intermediate System for Motion Picture Film", 100:156, March 1991.

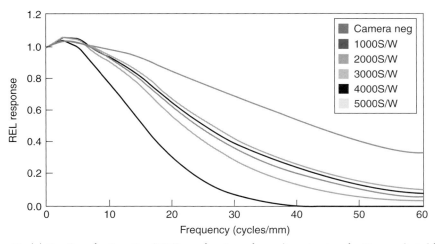

Figure 6-4. Modulation Transfer Function (MTF) as a function of sampling structure for Cineon digital film system.

on a 35 mm Academy aperture. For reference, the MTF of a camera negative, which includes the negative film and camera lens, is also shown. MTF curves representing an analog photochemical system do not give you a single number to judge the resolution of film. If one takes a middle frequency of 25 cycles per mm as a basis, you can see that the system MTF response increases from about 15% at 1K to 40% at 2K and about 50% at 3K and 53% at 4K. So the system MTF improves significantly as the sampling resolution is increased from 1K to 2K, with diminishing returns beyond that. Kodak decided to design its Cineon system with a base resolution of 4096 samples per picture width. With a nod towards practical and cost-effective post production work, however, Kodak also provided a direct 2K mode. Even today, more than 10 years later, nearly all visual effects are done at 2K resolution.

Kodak's analysis included the input camera negative film and the output inter-negative element. It modeled the aperture response of the CCD film scanner and the Gaussian spot of the laser film recorder. It did not include the print film or the film projector, both of which further reduce the system MTF. Original negative films improved substantially in the last 15 years, now exhibiting higher speed and lower grain. However, the MTF has not improved much, and typical camera lenses are the same, and today's CCD film scanners and laser film recorders have similar MTF characteristics as the original Cineon scanners and recorders.

So, if the system MTF improvement between 2K and 4K is on the order of 25% and the increase in cost is about 50%, why would anyone want to work in 4K? The strongest reason is that many want to see a digital cinema distribution system that is capable of producing substantially sharper pictures than high definition television, even if this cannot be realized today with 35 mm film origination.

In fact, the sharpness of some 1080p high definition television displays in the home is substantially better than a traditional 35 mm release print.

Even with an optically band-limited system like a camera negative (filtered by the camera lens and the MTF response of the film), it is still desirable to over-sample the picture to avoid aliasing. In fact, scanning at 4K, then filtering and down-sampling the image to 2K, produces sharper pictures with less aliasing than a direct 2K scanning process. Likewise, over-sampling on the output can blend the structure of the image and reduce aliasing of high contrast edges, particularly on diagonal lines and graphics or fonts. So, even if the digital master is produced at 2K resolution, there are good reasons to scan it at 4K, "down-rez" it for 2K manipulation, then "up-rez" it to 4K for film recording.

Some studios may be willing to pay extra for a 4K digital intermediate just to have it for available for those screens that are equipped with 4K digital cinema projectors. At the time of this writing, Sony has just introduced a 4K SXRD digital cinema projector, although only a small number are currently installed in commercial cinemas. There may also be some value in archiving a 4K digital master to protect for future release options.

It is important, however, to remember the DCI position that both 2K and 4K digital cinema exhibition will be supported by all studios. This means that exhibitors are free to make their own choice of projectors and manufacturer, balancing reliability and operating cost with all aspects of picture quality including resolution, without fear of obsolescence. Studios can chose to distribute their movies in either 2K or 4K packages. The servers must be able to ingest and store either 2K or 4K masters, playing back the appropriate resolution required for the installed projector. By affirming the DCI specification, the participating studios all committed to delivering movies to screens equipped with either 2K or 4K projectors, allowing exhibitors to make that choice.

Film-centric Workflow

With film prints being the primary distribution medium today, it makes sense that most digital intermediate processes follow a film-centric model, with film input and film output, and use a film-compatible digital file format—DPX or Cineon. In these file formats, the picture is stored as a digital representation of the camera negative film, in 10-bit logarithmic printing density, as described in Chapter 2. Since this is a low-contrast negative representation, the picture must be printed to impart the desired contrast and color space. To provide for interactive display during color grading, a 3D color LUT is used to emulate the characteristics of the print film. At the time of this publication, tools to build these color LUTs are available from Arri, Filmlight, Imagica, Kodak, Rising Sun and Thomson. Real-time 3D-LUT boxes (with dual-link SMPTE 292M inputs and outputs) are available from Filmlight, Kodak and Thomson.

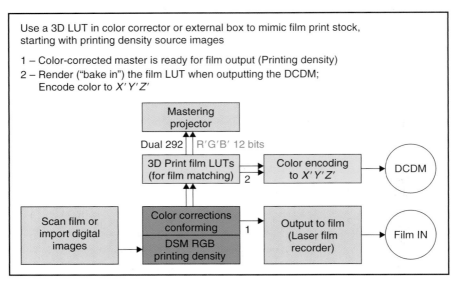

Figure 6-5. DI-Film-centric Method.

This film-centric process is illustrated in Figure 6.5. When the digital master has been conformed and graded, it is ready for film output with no additional conversion steps required since the working file format is the same as that used by digital film recorders. However, the digital cinema distribution master requires one additional step. The same 3D color LUT that was used to emulate print film in the color grading process must be rendered or "baked" into the DCDM files. This process can be combined with the color space conversion to X'Y'Z', so that both are implemented in one combined 3D Color LUT.

Another aspect of the film centric approach is the need to "scan and protect" the full camera aperture and to carry it through to the film output. Although the standard "Academy" projection aperture is 1.85:1, not that different from the 1.78:1 HD displays or the 1.89:1 native aspect ratio of digital cinema projectors, the original camera aperture is 1.37:1. By scanning and protecting the full camera aperture, its means that the digital inter-negative produced at the end of the process has frames with the same aspect ratio (1.37) as a conventional inter-negative. More importantly, since home video distribution has access to a full-frame image for conversion to standard definition, the traditional full-frame (1.33:1) home video master can simply be a down-conversion from the digital master without any reframing needed. This assumes, of course, that the cinematographer also protected the full height of the camera aperture during the original photography, insuring that sound booms and lighting fixtures are kept out of frame.

For pictures shot with anamorphic lenses for wide-screen presentation, this scan and protect approach is even more important. Cinemascope™ was developed in the 1950's as response to the impending threat of television. It provided a clever way to create wide-screen (2.39:1) pictures while still backward-compatible with standard 35 mm film, cameras, printers and projectors. The cinemascope camera lenses squeeze the image horizontally by a factor of two, fitting it into the full height of the camera aperture, and an inverse lens expands the picture at the projector. The advantage of doing it this way, rather than just letterboxing the frame within the standard Academy aperture is that it utilizes nearly 50% more negative area, producing pictures that are sharper and finer grain. It also is more efficient optically, allowing projectors to fill a wider screen with the same lamp that is used for a 1.85:1 presentation.

If the intended release is a widescreen 2.39:1 format, then the highest quality method is to shoot the film anamorphically, scan the full aperture height, carry this full height through the digital mastering process, and output to an anamorphic frame on the inter-negative. This captures the sharpness and lower grain advantages associated with the largest possible film area. For grading purposes, the picture is digitally squeezed by 50% vertically and letterboxed for square-pixel display, eliminating the need for an anamorphic projection lens. Since the 2.39:1 Digital Cinema Distribution Master calls for a 2048 (2K) × 858 or 4096 (4K) × 1714 square-pixel format for distribution, the same scaling is used to create the DCDM, although it is not necessary to actually pad the top and bottom of the frame with null data.

Format	Horizontal	Vertical	Camera Aspect Ratio	Projection Aspect Ratio
Academy	3656	2664	1.37	1.85
Cinemascope	3656	3112	1.175	2.39
Full Aperture	4096	3112	1.32	2.39
DCDM-4K	3996	2160	NA	1.85
DCDM-4K	4096	1716	NA	2.39

Table 6-A. Scanned Resolutions and Aspect Ratios for common 35 mm Film Formats, compared to the 4K Image Structure for the Digital Cinema Distribution Master, DCDM. Note that the Scanned Resolutions correspond to the Camera Aperture, and that the Projection Aperture is smaller.

Super-35 is a popular alternative for producing widescreen 2.39:1 pictures and has been bolstered by the advantage of digital scaling as part of the digital intermediate process. It starts with capturing a full-aperture 35 mm frame that covers perforation to perforation. It makes use of standard 35 mm spherical camera lenses which includes fast primes and zooms that are not available in anamorphic camera lenses. When this format was first introduced, it required an optical printing step to extract a 2.39:1 image from the full-aperture negative and stretch it vertically 2:1 to create an anamorphic inter-positive. This extra lens softened the image, and flare reduced the contrast. However, with digital intermediate, it is a trivial extra step to resize the picture for anamorphic output. Most importantly, the resulting picture is much sharper and does not lose contrast. In fact, since spherical prime lenses have better MTF and lateral color characteristics than anamorphic camera lenses, some even say that these pictures are sharper even than traditional anamorphic photography. However, Super-35 pictures are still visibly grainier, since the negative area is approximately 35% less than that of the anamorphic frame.

In the film-centric approach, computer-generated or digitally captured images must be converted into a logarithmic printing density space for combination with film. If the difference in color sensitivities is ignored, than this is simply a set of three 1-D lookup tables. This is typically the approach taken in visual effects.

Camera vs. Projection Aperture

The traditional practice in film scanning and recording is to scan and reproduce the camera aperture, so that the image remains the same size on the inter-negative as the original negative without re-sampling, and the resulting print can be projected with a standard projection aperture. The standard film projection aperture is 5% smaller than the camera aperture, providing some margin for hiding the frame lines, covering any dirt caught in the camera aperture and also providing some "wiggle room" for picture weave (unsteadiness) introduced due to mechanical tolerances in printing and projection. This practice works fine for film projection.

However, the Digital Cinema Distribution Master does not distinguish between the image size of the master and the display. In fact, the DCI specification explicitly states that the projector must be capable of displaying the full DCDM, pixel for pixel, without any cropping. So, what happens if the digital cinema master is produced from the full width of the camera aperture? If the camera aperture is uneven or dirty, this distracting impairment may be visible on the digital projector, depending on the adjustment of the masking. With most theatres equipped with variable masking, it is standard practice to bring the masking into the picture area a little to provide a good clean black boundary to the picture. But this may not be enough.

One option is to re-size the picture for the DCDM, pushing in so that 95% of the original scan (1946 pixels wide) is resized to 2048 pixels wide, insuring that the digital picture is projected at the same size as the film print. However, this means that all DCDMs will suffer a small sharpness loss due to the 5% enlargement. Although this is probably acceptable operationally, it is inconsistent with the objective of optimizing the quality of the digital cinema presentation.

At the time of this writing, another alternative is being discussed. Basically, the idea is to define a digital projection aperture of 2000 pixels in width, similar to the projection aperture plates used in film cameras. The digital projection aperture need only be 2.5% smaller than the DCDM image size, rather than the nominal 5% of the film projection aperture, because digital projection systems do not have to contend with the unsteadiness inherent in the film printing and projection processes.

THE DIGITAL MASTERING PROCESS FOR STEM

The Standard Evaluation Material (StEM) was scripted, designed, photographed and directed by volunteers from the American Society of Cinematographers (ASC) with technical support from DCI. The StEM movie is a 12 minute short film that follows an Italian wedding party through several scenes from mid-day through night, to include a wide range of lighting conditions. DCI paid for the production and post production of this film so that the movie could be assembled for digital cinema testing, and that it could be made widely available to manufacturers and service providers in the industry.

Figure 6-6.   The mid-day wedding party scene from the ASC/DCI Standard Evaluation Material (StEM).

The goal was to produce pictorial evaluation material that could be used for testing all aspects of digital cinema distribution, including comparing projection with film display, verifying the color conversion steps, and evaluating compression artifacts. As such, it included many elements that had proven troublesome in past testing of digital compression or display systems, such as confetti, torches, jugglers, rotating bicycle wheels, camera pans, and fog effects. Although 35 mm anamorphic was the principal film format used for origination, it was supplemented by some shots on Super-35 and 65 mm (5-perf). Kodak Vision 5218 (EI 400) was the primary film stock used, with one daylight scene shot on fine-grain Kodak 5245 (EI 50). No digital cameras were used for origination, because at the time (August 2003) the new film-style digital cameras were still in prototype form.

Although the DCI requirements were pushing the edge of available post production tools at the end of 2003, the workflow was designed to demonstrate a complete digital cinema mastering approach. Many more tools are available today that support digital cinema mastering and some of the workarounds are no longer necessary, but the basic

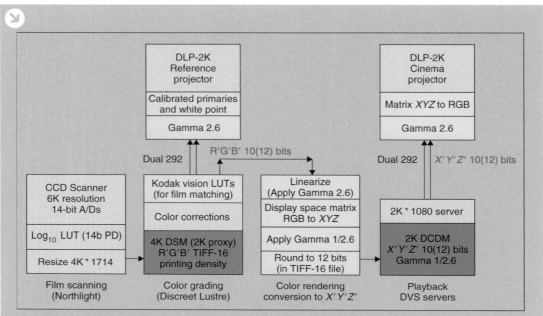

Figure 6-7.   Flow Chart for StEM Post Production.

digital intermediate process that was used for the StEM movie is still a useful case study. A flow chart that shows the processing steps is shown in Figure 6.7.

The film was telecined for HD dailies and then edited using Apple's Final Cut Pro. Once the edit was approved, negative pull lists were generated for scanning. Because the required output was both 4K and 2K DCDMs, the decision was made to scan the film at the highest resolution available (6K for 35 mm), which at the time dictated the choice of the Northlight™ film scanner. Furthermore, since the DCDM required 12 bits per color, and since the normal mode of the scanner was 10-bit printing density in DPX files, the scanner was set up to output 14-bit linear data directly from its A/D Converter, with external black and gain corrections and conversion to 14 bit log data. A bi-cubic filter was used for resizing from 6K to 4K (4096 x 1714 for the 2.39:1 aspect ratio). Since there are no 14 bit file formats, and since 12-bit DPX modes were not supported by any commercially available tools, the 14 bit picture data was stored in 16-bit TIFF files. Interestingly, the only available 65 mm scanner (Imagica) at the time had a maximum resolution of 4K and could only output 10-bit log data, so this was what was used for the 65 mm scenes.

A traditional film answer print was produced by FotoKem to provide a reference for color and other image quality attributes. Cinematographer Alan Daviau supervised the answer printing, and then returned to guide the digital color grading process. A Discreet Lustre™ color corrector was used for the digital color grading. The color corrector was installed in the middle of the auditorium at the Digital Cinema Lab in Hollywood, so that the digital picture could be graded side by side with the projected film answer print. A Kinoton 35 mm film projector with an electronic transport was used, because it could be run slowly and even rewound without threading. A Christie CP2000™ DLP Cinema® projector calibrated to the DCI primaries and white point was used for the digital display.

Within the Lustre file system, 2K and 1K proxies were generated from the original files for interactive color correction. End credits were generated at 4K and imported. The Lustre was also used to render dissolves and to conform the shots to the EDL. A plug-in 3D color LUT from Kodak was used in the display path to emulate Vision Print Film 5383. With this display LUT, it was possible to perform most of the color corrections as basic RGB "printer light" corrections, with some adjustment of whites and blacks. The digital projector (with a contrast ratio of 1800:1 as measured off the screen) had plenty of range to match the blacks of the projected film print. Most importantly, with the 3D color LUT, no secondary color corrections were necessary. Once the color grading was completed on the proxies, the 4K source files were rendered, with the Vision print LUT rendered into the color-corrected files.

The color conversion to $X'Y'Z'$ was accomplished using Apple's Shake™ software. The digital files were linearized (applying a gamma of 2.6), then a 3x3 matrix was applied to convert RGB to XYZ, followed by application of the 1/2.6 gamma function. The finished color-corrected files were stored as 12-bit $X'Y'Z'$ data in 16-bit TIFF files. This process will be described in more detail in Chapter 7.

For playback, the 4K StEM files were re-sampled to 2K (using a bi-cubic filter) and loaded unto a DVS Clipster™ disk recorder for playback. The DVS Clipster™ was selected because, at the time, it was the only storage device that supported 12-bit output through dual-link SMPTE 372M. DVS now supplies these output cards to other vendors of color correction equipment.

For display of $X'Y'Z'$ color data, Texas Instruments provided a custom linear color space conversion matrix that transformed the linearized XYZ code values to the native RGB of the Christie CP2000™ DLP Cinema® projectors in the digital cinema lab. This capability has since been incorporated in all DLP Cinema® projectors. The StEM movie was shown in multiple configurations.

First, the RGB digital master was played back split-screen with the film answer print, with the digital picture inverted left-to-right, creating a "butterfly" comparison of the same part of the picture. With the exception of a deep cyan in the foggy night scene, the color reproduction of the digital cinema system closely matched the film answer print, and shadows and highlights were faithfully reproduced without any loss of detail. Many observers commented that the digital picture was sharper and cleaner (less grain) than the film answer print. It was also noticeably steadier and flicker-less, although it should be noted that the Kinoton projector is renowned for its steadiness and uniformity. The unsteadiness and flicker are only really significant when showcased split-screen with a superior digital projector. The only objection that some observers offered to the digital picture was the appearance of some structure or "screen door" artifacts when the picture was viewed from the front row of seats (approx. 1 screen height).

The second screening test with the StEM movie was to compare R′G′B′ to $X'Y'Z'$ color files to prove that the color transformations were implemented correctly and that no contouring or other artifacts were introduced in the process. The original R′G′B′ master was loaded on one DVS Clipster™ unit and displayed on one Christie CP2000™ DLP Cinema® projector. The color-converted $X'Y'Z'$ files were loaded onto the other Clipster™ and displayed on the second projector. The projected pictures were compared in a split-screen, butterfly presentation. This test showed that the two pictures matched very, very closely (within the calibration tolerances of the white point) and that there were no contouring or other artifacts in the $X'Y'Z'$ data.

Finally, the third screening test was to simulate 4K pictures by loading the 4K $X'Y'Z'$ data onto two Clipster™ units, with the 4K picture split into left and right half pictures and cropped vertically from 1714 to 1080 lines, and projected on the two Christie CP2000™ projectors with long-throw lenses. In addition, 4K was compared to the mirrored half of a 2K frame (using the standard lens). Some observers commented that the 4K picture looked impressive, with no visible structure unless you walked up to the screen to study it closely. It can be noted, however, that the pictures were essentially the same when viewed from a distance of more than two picture heights, where the structure of the 2K picture was also invisible.

Digital-centric Workflow

As digital cinema distribution takes hold, and as digital cameras become more popular, it is likely that the digital intermediate process will migrate from a film-centric approach to one more consistent with the digital input and output formats. This is only natural as the digital inputs and outputs become the primary vehicles for origination and distribution. This will have significant internal ramifications for facilities providing digital intermediate services, but if done correctly, should be transparent to the customer. The cardinal rule is "what you see (and sign off on) is

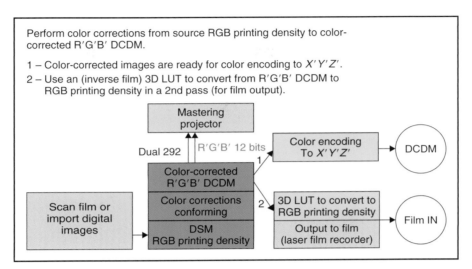

Figure 6-8. DI-Digital-centric Method.

what you get". In other words, it is the facility's responsibility to calibrate their color correction system, reference displays and film or digital output, so that all outputs look the same as the picture on the reference display.

Instead of working in logarithmic printing density, some facilities may chose to work in a linear RGB color space, importing digital camera or film images through a 1-D LUT that converts the pictures to scene-referred linear color space. The controls of the color corrector would need to be recalibrated to work on linear signals (rather than gamma-corrected or log signals), and an output gamma correction of approximately 0.6 applied so that the net system gamma on the 2.6 gamma digital cinema reference display is about 1.5. There is no need for the 3-D color LUT that emulates print film, because the picture on the reference projector is now the primary deliverable. It is a simple step to encode the color from RGB to X'Y'Z' for the DCDM. However, for the film output, it is now necessary to build an inverse 3-D color LUT that compensates for the inter-dependent characteristics of color print film. This is illustrated in Figure 6.8. Since the digital projector is capable of producing much brighter primary colors, it will be necessary to include some gamut mapping to avoid contouring. A basic approach to gamut mapping will be discussed in Chapter 8.

7

Color Encoding for Digital Cinema Distribution

This chapter will describe the derivation of the color encoding and decoding matrices for digital cinema distribution. By the nature of the matrix math involved it is somewhat technical and probably of most interest to those interested in delving into the theory behind the color conversions.

The X'Y'Z' DCDM encoding is a non-linear encoding, but it is based on the XYZ linear, additive, color encoding system defined by the CIE in 1931. Television is also a non-linear R'G'B' encoding that is based on an RGB linear, additive, imaging system. The mathematics of dealing with color conversions between different additive display devices, whether television or digital cinema devices, is the same. The concepts involved are straightforward, but the math can be confusing due to the number of steps needed to calculate the different transforms. Although the calculations described in SMPTE Documents RP 176 and RP 177 are explicitly for television systems, the calculations apply equally well to the transformations between the DCDM encoding and any real, additive, display device.

The derivations of the color conversion matrices will be reviewed here and a specific numerical example will be worked. These equations apply to any additive digital cinema display. In practical application, there is some deviation from these equations in the lowest luminance region. In that region because light energy is additive, a small amount of stray light or flare light will alter the result predicted by these equations. However, a simple modification to the equations, the addition of the XYZ tristimulus values of the stray light, will significantly improve the accuracy of these equations. In this discussion, that stray light will assumed to be absent.

There are two laws of colorimetry upon which the DCDM encoding is based and which are the starting points for all of the following calculations:

1   If two light sources have the same CIE 1931 tristimulus values in the same viewing environment, these two light sources will appear the same to an observer with normal color vision.

2   When one light source with CIE tristimulus values XYZ_1 is added to a second light source with CIE tristimulus values XYZ_2, the tristimulus values for the combination of these two spectral distributions is $XYZ_1 + XYZ_2$.

There are two other points that must be made in order to understand the following equations. The first point is that in all of these equations, the XYZ and RGB values are normalized values, which means they range in value from 0 to 1. In many applications, the normalized values are needed. In other applications, the absolute values are needed. The conversion from the normalized to the absolute values is a multiplication operation—multiplication of the normalized values by the appropriate constant. Therefore, although the following equations make use of the normalized XYZ and RGB values, it is left to the user to determine whether normalized or absolute values are needed in a particular piece of equipment.

The second point is that it is assumed that the light output of the display device that is represented by these equations has a light output that is directly proportional to the RGB values. There are cases in which this is not true. For example, a television with a power supply too small for the television may be able to produce a small very bright red or green or blue pixel or area of pixels, but when the entire television screen is white, the power supply may not have enough power to produce a white that is as bright as the sum of the red alone plus the green alone plus the blue alone.

SMPTE RP 176 describes the basic color conversion equations. There are two general equations. Equation 1 comes from Section 5.1 of RP 176

$$\begin{pmatrix} X \\ Y \\ Z \end{pmatrix} = \begin{pmatrix} X_R & X_G & X_B \\ Y_R & Y_G & Y_B \\ Z_R & Z_G & Z_B \end{pmatrix} \times \begin{pmatrix} R \\ G \\ B \end{pmatrix} = \text{NPM} \times \begin{pmatrix} R \\ G \\ B \end{pmatrix} \tag{1}$$

where XYZ are the CIE tristimulus values, and the R, G, B sub-scripts refer to the Red, Green, and Blue primaries. RGB are the normalized linear RGB video levels. In a more general system, RGB are the normalized linear levels or normalized linear amounts of each of the primaries. NPM is the normalized primary matrix.

Equation 2 comes from Section 5.2 of RP 176:

$$\begin{pmatrix} R \\ G \\ B \end{pmatrix} = NPM^{-1} \times \begin{pmatrix} X \\ Y \\ Z \end{pmatrix} \qquad (2)$$

Equation 1 shows how to go from the RGB values to the XYZ tristimulus values and Equation 2 shows how to go from the XYZ tristimulus values to the RGB values.

Section 5.4 states, "These normalized linear RGB values are then transformed to the nonlinear R'G'B' relative video levels using the opto-electronic transfer function." In the general system, the linear RGB values are transformed to the nonlinear R'G'B' values by the defined non-linear transfer function. For the DCDM encoding, this is the 1/2.6 gamma described in Chapter 4.

Although RP 176 says that the NPM is calculated from six colors and a white, it does not say how that is done. RP 177 gives the specifics on how to calculate the NPM. What follows is a summary of the equations and calculations in RP 177.

Section 3.3.1 of RP 177 says to obtain the CIE x, y chromaticity coordinates of the reference white and of the Red, Green, and Blue primaries. Section 3.3.2 says to compute the z coordinate for the reference white and each of the RGB primaries:

$$z = 1 - (x + y) \qquad (3)$$

Section 3.3.3 specifies that to form the following P matrix and W column vector from the $[x\ y\ z]$ chromaticity coordinates of the Red, Green, and Blue primaries and reference white:

$$P = \begin{pmatrix} x_R & x_G & x_B \\ y_R & y_G & y_B \\ z_R & z_G & z_B \end{pmatrix} \qquad (4)$$

$$W = \begin{pmatrix} x_W/y_W \\ 1 \\ z_W/y_W \end{pmatrix} \qquad (5)$$

where the R, G, and B subscripts have the same meaning as in Equation 1 and the W subscript refers to the reference white.

Section 3.3.3 says that the W vector, representing the reference white, has been normalized so that white has a luminance factor of 1.0, i.e. $Y = 1.0$. This is necessary so as to cause the video reference white signal (R = G = B = 1) to produce the reference white with a unity luminance factor. This is equally true for the DCDM encoding. The normalized reference white signal (R = G = B = 1) must produce the reference white with a unity luminance factor in the DCDM.

Section 3.3.4 says to compute the elements of a vector by multiplying the W vector by the inverse of the P matrix. The notation P^{-1} indicates the matrix inversion operation. These C_R, C_G, and C_B elements are normalization factors that normalize the intensities of the Red, Green, and Blue primaries such that a unit amount of each primary combine to produce the white point chromaticities with a luminance factor of 1:

$$\begin{pmatrix} C_R \\ C_G \\ C_B \end{pmatrix} = P^{-1} \times W \tag{6}$$

Section 3.3.5 says to form the diagonal matrix from the vector elements C_R, C_G, and C_B:

$$C = \begin{pmatrix} C_R & 0 & 0 \\ 0 & C_G & 0 \\ 0 & 0 & C_B \end{pmatrix} \tag{7}$$

Section 3.3.6 says to compute the final normalized primary matrix NPM as the product of the P and C matrices:

$$NPM = \begin{pmatrix} X_R & X_G & X_B \\ Y_R & Y_G & Y_B \\ Z_R & Z_G & Z_B \end{pmatrix} = P \times C \tag{8}$$

Section 3.3.7 says that this matrix, NPM, is the final result and relates television linear RGB signals to CIE XYZ tristimulus values as follows:

$$\begin{pmatrix} X \\ Y \\ Z \end{pmatrix} = \begin{pmatrix} X_R & X_G & X_B \\ Y_R & Y_G & Y_B \\ Z_R & Z_G & Z_B \end{pmatrix} \times \begin{pmatrix} R \\ G \\ B \end{pmatrix} = NPM \times \begin{pmatrix} R \\ G \\ B \end{pmatrix} \tag{9}$$

Equation 9 is the same equation as Equation 1.

Section 4 describes the equations to transform from one primary set to another. Section 4.1 says that the input data consists of the normalized primary matrices for a source system (NPM$_S$) and for a destination system (NPM$_D$). Note that although the RP says this is a transform between primary sets, the NPM matrices contain information from both the primaries and the white point of each system. The equations are equally valid for transforms between (1) different primaries with the same white points, (2) the same primaries with different white points, and (3) different primaries with different white points.

Section 4.2.1 says that given the normalized primary matrices for the source (NPM$_S$) and the destination (NPM$_D$) systems, the following equations relate CIE tristimulus values to the linear RGB signals in both source and destination systems:

$$\begin{pmatrix} X \\ Y \\ Z \end{pmatrix} = NPM_S \times \begin{pmatrix} R_S \\ G_S \\ B_S \end{pmatrix} \tag{10a}$$

$$\begin{pmatrix} X \\ Y \\ Z \end{pmatrix} = NPM_D \times \begin{pmatrix} R_D \\ G_D \\ B_D \end{pmatrix} \tag{10b}$$

The inverse relationships, predicting RGB from XYZ, may also be written:

$$\begin{pmatrix} R_S \\ G_S \\ B_S \end{pmatrix} = NPM_S^{-1} \times \begin{pmatrix} X \\ Y \\ Z \end{pmatrix} \tag{11a}$$

$$\begin{pmatrix} R_D \\ G_D \\ B_D \end{pmatrix} = NPM_D^{-1} \times \begin{pmatrix} X \\ Y \\ Z \end{pmatrix} \tag{11b}$$

Again, the (−1) notation of the NPM matrices indicates matrix inversion.

Section 4.2.2 defines how to determine a matrix that transforms RGB signals from the source system into appropriate signals for the destination system. Equation 12a shows how to predict XYZ values from the source RGB signal values. Equation 12b predicts the destination RGB signals from the XYZ values.

$$\begin{pmatrix} X \\ Y \\ Z \end{pmatrix} = NPM_S \times \begin{pmatrix} R_S \\ G_S \\ B_S \end{pmatrix} \tag{12a}$$

$$\begin{pmatrix} R \\ G \\ B \end{pmatrix} = NPM_D^{-1} \times \begin{pmatrix} X \\ Y \\ Z \end{pmatrix} \tag{12b}$$

Since the values of XYZ are the same for both source and destination systems when the color displayed is the same, the XYZ vector on the right side of Equation 12b can be replaced with the entire right side of Equation 12a

$$\begin{pmatrix} R_D \\ G_D \\ B_D \end{pmatrix} = NPM_D^{-1} \times NPM_S \times \begin{pmatrix} R_S \\ G_S \\ B_S \end{pmatrix} \tag{13}$$

Section 4.2.3 says that the desired transformation matrix TRA is the product of NPM_D inverse and NPM_S:

$$TRA = NPM_D^{-1} \times NPM_S \tag{14}$$

and

$$\begin{pmatrix} R_D \\ G_D \\ B_D \end{pmatrix} = TRA \times \begin{pmatrix} R_S \\ G_S \\ B_S \end{pmatrix} \tag{15}$$

Annexes B and C of RP 177 provide some numerical examples. The recommendation in the RPs is to use 10 significant digits in the matrices and round the RGB or XYZ values to four significant digits after computing them to 10 significant digits. Although the use of 10 significant digits in the matrices will eliminate round-off errors, matrices calculated from measurements will not have 10 significant digits of accuracy.

Although RP 176 and RP 177 were written for television applications, the equations derived and described above are equally applicable to the D-Cinema system. In the following paragraphs, the use of these same equations in the D-Cinema system will be described.

Table 7-A shows the chromaticity coordinates of the DCDM encoding primaries and the DCDM encoding white point, along with the Reference Projector primaries and white point. These are the chromaticity coordinates that will be used in the calculations that follow.

Color	DCDM Encoding		Reference Projector	
	x	y	x	y
Red Primary	1.0000	0.0000	0.6800	0.3200
Green Primary	0.0000	1.0000	0.2650	0.6900
Blue Primary	0.0000	0.0000	0.1500	0.0600
White	0.3333	0.3333	0.3140	0.3510

Table 7-A. Chromaticity coordinates of the primaries and white points of the DCDM encoding and the Reference Projector.

Using the chromaticity coordinates in Table 2, the NPM matrices for both systems can be calculated using the equations above. In these calculations, the subscript DCDM refers to the DCDM encoding and the subscript RP refers to the Reference Projector system.

From Equation 4:

$$P_{DCDM} = \begin{vmatrix} 1.0000 & 0.0000 & 0.0000 \\ 0.0000 & 1.0000 & 0.0000 \\ 0.0000 & 0.0000 & 1.0000 \end{vmatrix} \tag{16}$$

$$P_{RP} = \begin{vmatrix} 0.6800 & 0.2650 & 0.1500 \\ 0.3200 & 0.6900 & 0.0600 \\ 0.0000 & 0.0450 & 0.7900 \end{vmatrix} \tag{17}$$

From Equation 5:

$$W_{DCDM} = \begin{vmatrix} 1.0000 \\ 1.0000 \\ 1.0000 \end{vmatrix} \tag{18}$$

$$W_{RP} = \begin{vmatrix} 0.8946 \\ 1.0000 \\ 0.9544 \end{vmatrix} \tag{19}$$

From Equations 6 and 7:

$$C_{DCDM} = \begin{vmatrix} 1.0000 & 0.0000 & 0.0000 \\ 0.0000 & 1.0000 & 0.0000 \\ 0.0000 & 0.0000 & 1.0000 \end{vmatrix} \tag{20}$$

$$C_{RP} = \begin{vmatrix} 0.6547 & 0.0000 & 0.0000 \\ 0.0000 & 1.0158 & 0.0000 \\ 0.0000 & 0.0000 & 1.1486 \end{vmatrix} \tag{21}$$

From Equation 8

$$NPM_{DCDM} = \begin{vmatrix} 1.0000 & 0.0000 & 0.0000 \\ 0.0000 & 1.0000 & 0.0000 \\ 0.0000 & 0.0000 & 1.0000 \end{vmatrix} \tag{22}$$

$$\text{NPM}_{RP} = \begin{pmatrix} 0.4452 & 0.2771 & 0.1723 \\ 0.2095 & 0.7216 & 0.0689 \\ 0.0000 & 0.0471 & 0.9074 \end{pmatrix} \tag{23}$$

From Equation 9 for the DCDM system:

$$\begin{pmatrix} X \\ Y \\ Z \end{pmatrix} = \begin{pmatrix} 1.0000 & 0.0000 & 0.0000 \\ 0.0000 & 1.0000 & 0.0000 \\ 0.0000 & 0.0000 & 1.0000 \end{pmatrix} \times \begin{pmatrix} R_{DCDM} \\ G_{DCDM} \\ B_{DCDM} \end{pmatrix} \tag{24}$$

For the Reference Projector system, Equation 9 is:

$$\begin{pmatrix} X \\ Y \\ Z \end{pmatrix} = \begin{pmatrix} 0.4452 & 0.2771 & 0.1723 \\ 0.2095 & 0.7216 & 0.0689 \\ 0.0000 & 0.0471 & 0.9074 \end{pmatrix} \times \begin{pmatrix} R_{RP} \\ G_{RP} \\ B_{RP} \end{pmatrix} \tag{25}$$

For the DCDM system, Equations 2 and 11 are:

$$\begin{pmatrix} R_{DCDM} \\ G_{DCDM} \\ B_{DCDM} \end{pmatrix} = \begin{pmatrix} 1.0000 & 0.0000 & 0.0000 \\ 0.0000 & 1.0000 & 0.0000 \\ 0.0000 & 0.0000 & 1.0000 \end{pmatrix} \times \begin{pmatrix} X \\ Y \\ Z \end{pmatrix} \tag{26}$$

Likewise, for the Reference Projector system, the corresponding equation is:

$$\begin{pmatrix} R_{RP} \\ G_{RP} \\ B_{RP} \end{pmatrix} = \begin{pmatrix} 2.7254 & -1.0180 & -0.4402 \\ -0.7952 & 1.6897 & -0.0226 \\ 0.0412 & -0.0876 & 1.1009 \end{pmatrix} \times \begin{pmatrix} X \\ Y \\ Z \end{pmatrix} \tag{27}$$

Because in Equations 24 and 26 the NPM and the inverse of NPM are unity matrices, RGB = XYZ in the DCDM system. Therefore, although it is correct to call the DCDM system an XYZ system, it is really an RGB system that follows all the equations that people have been using with RGB systems, but it is a special case of an RGB system due to the primaries – the primaries of the CIE 1931 system, and white point – the Equal Energy white point. The Reference Projector system, as shown by Equations 25 and 27, is mathematically more difficult to work with than the DCDM system because the matrices are not unity matrices. The Reference Projector system is mathematically similar to the conventional television system – only the numbers in the NPM and inverse NPM matrices are different. By using Equations 25 and 26 and Equations 24 and 27, we can derive the relationships between the DCDM and the Reference Projector systems:

$$\begin{pmatrix} R_{DCDM} \\ G_{DCDM} \\ B_{DCDM} \end{pmatrix} = \begin{pmatrix} 0.4452 & 0.2771 & 0.1723 \\ 0.2095 & 0.7216 & 0.0689 \\ 0.0000 & 0.0471 & 0.9074 \end{pmatrix} \times \begin{pmatrix} R_{RP} \\ G_{RP} \\ B_{RP} \end{pmatrix} \tag{28}$$

$$\begin{pmatrix} R_{RP} \\ G_{RP} \\ B_{RP} \end{pmatrix} = \begin{pmatrix} 2.7254 & -1.0180 & -0.4402 \\ -0.7952 & 1.6897 & -0.0226 \\ 0.0412 & -0.0876 & 1.1009 \end{pmatrix} - \begin{pmatrix} R_{DCDM} \\ G_{DCDM} \\ B_{DCDM} \end{pmatrix} \tag{29}$$

It must be remembered that these equations apply to the RGB values that are the linear normalized values, not the gamma encoded values. The RGB_{DCDM} values are the CIE XYZ values.

Color Conversion to XYZ

Color conversion from R′G′B′ to X′Y′Z′ requires a three-step process which involves linearizing the color-corrected R′G′B′ signals (by applying a 2.6 gamma function), followed by their passage through a linear 3 × 3 transform matrix. The resultant linearized and coded XYZ signals are then given an inverse 2.6 gamma transfer characteristic whose output is quantized to 12 bits.

Note that the transfer function of the Reference Projector is specified to be Gamma 2.6 (explicitly) and that the actual coefficients of the color transform matrices depend on the color primaries of the Mastering Projector (encoding side) and the Cinema Projector (decoding side), and their respective white points.

The processing steps for converting the R′G′B′ code values (which range from 0 to 4095) of the color-graded master to device-independent X′Y′Z′ are shown below. This color space conversion can be implemented within the color corrector or applied in a separate batch process. First, the R′G′B′ data is linearized by applying a simple gamma 2.6 transfer function:

$$R = \left(\frac{R'}{4095} \right)^{2.6}, \text{ and likewise for G and B.}$$

The output (RGB) of this linearization is a floating point number that ranges from 0 to 1.0. The 3 × 3 linear matrix is then applied to this signal, resulting in another linear XYZ signal with floating point values that range from 0 to 1.0. To minimize quantization errors, this matrix should be implemented as a floating point calculation.

$$\begin{pmatrix} X \\ Y \\ Z \end{pmatrix} = \begin{pmatrix} 0.4452 & 0.2771 & 0.1723 \\ 0.2095 & 0.7216 & 0.0689 \\ 0.0000 & 0.0471 & 0.9074 \end{pmatrix} \times \begin{pmatrix} R_{DC} \\ G_{DC} \\ B_{DC} \end{pmatrix}$$

Finally, the X'Y'Z' encoding transfer function is defined by the following expression. Please note that this equation does not compensate for the screen black level, so it represents a relative encoding of the luminance values above the screen black level.[1] In this expression, X is a floating point number between 0 and 1.0, and the output $CV_{X'}$ is an integer ranging between 0 and 4095.

$$CV_{X'} = INT\left[4095 \times \left(\frac{X}{52.37}\right)^{1/2.6}\right], \text{ and likewise for Y and Z}$$

The inverse X'Y'Z'-to-RGB processing steps for a Digital Cinema Projector with the same color primaries as the Reference Projector (subscript DC) are shown below, where the projector transfer function is a pure 2.6 gamma power law as defined in section 7.9.[2]

$$X'Y'Z' \xrightarrow{2.6} XYZ \xrightarrow{[\ ]} RGB \rightarrow \boxed{\text{Light Modulators}}$$

$$\begin{pmatrix} R_{DC} \\ G_{DC} \\ B_{DC} \end{pmatrix} = \begin{pmatrix} 2.7254 & -1.0180 & -0.4402 \\ -0.7952 & 1.6897 & -0.0226 \\ 0.0412 & -0.0876 & 1.1009 \end{pmatrix} \times \begin{pmatrix} X \\ Y \\ Z \end{pmatrix}$$

The above calculations showed how to go from the DCDM system to the Reference Projector system, but all in linear, normalized RGB values. The next section will show the calculations from the beginning to the end of the DCDM system. These calculations will follow the path starting at the DSM, go to linear XYZ values, go to the encoded DCDM X'Y'Z' values, go to linear XYZ values, and go to Reference Projector RGB values.

The Digital Source Master (DSM), and the way the image is encoded or displayed in the DSM, is not a part of the DCDM standards. The DSM may be encoded in different ways and that encoding

---

1. A more rigorous equation that describes the absolute on-screen luminance in the mastering environment is given by the following expression, where Screen Black Level (SBL) represents the black level measured off of the screen. Please note, that in practice, this equation is only used if the exhibition projector wants to attempt tone mapping, and if the mastering screen black level is provided in metadata.

$$CV_{X'} = INT\left[4095 \times \left(\frac{X - SBL_x}{52.37}\right)^{1/2.6}\right], \text{ and likewise for Y and Z.}$$

2. To rigorously reproduce the image as displayed in the mastering room, the exhibition projector must compensate for the difference between the screen black level in mastering and its own screen black level. Initial testing has shown that this compensation can result in undesirable clipping of some black detail when pictures are displayed on a lower contrast exhibition projector, and that in fact, the simple power law provides a natural (and forgiving) result.

may use different color spaces. How one converts from the DSM encoding to the XYZ values of any pixel depends on the approach. The XYZ values of each pixel are defined to be the XYZ values that the person saw on the screen at the time of approval of the content. This is called output-referred color encoding.

Computational Example

This chapter will end with an example that is numerically worked from beginning to end. First, let us assume that a person was looking at the monitor described in Annex A of SMPTE RP 176. We are not recommending that anyone use a monitor to preview material for display on a D-Cinema projector because the monitor's color gamut is smaller than the D-Cinema projector's color gamut. However, this numerical example uses both equations and numbers that are in SMPTE standards and thus makes the following calculations easier to follow. Consider only the red, green, and blue colors shown in Annex A of RP 176 and a 10% gray that will be calculated here. The NPM from RP 176 Annex A is

$$\text{NPM} = \begin{bmatrix} 0.4123907993 & 0.3575843394 & 0.180487884 \\ 0.2126390059 & 0.7151686788 & 0.0721923154 \\ 0.0193308187 & 0.1191947798 & 0.9505321522 \end{bmatrix} \tag{30}$$

Table B gives the RGB linear signals and the R′G′B′ non-linear RGB video signals. The RGB values for the three color patches came directly from Annex A of RP 176 and the RGB linear signals for the 10% gray are 10% of the values for the white. The R′G′B′ signals in Table 7-B were calculated from the equation in Annex A.

$$V' = 1.099 \times V^{0.45} - 0.099 \tag{31}$$

Using Equation 1 normalized XYZ values for these four patches were calculated from the RGB values in Table B. The equation to convert from normalized XYZ to absolute XYZ values is

$$\begin{bmatrix} X_{abs} \\ Y_{abs} \\ Z_{abs} \end{bmatrix} = 48.00 \times \begin{bmatrix} X_{norm} \\ Y_{norm} \\ Z_{norm} \end{bmatrix} \tag{32}$$

Patch	Linear RGB Values			Non-Linear R′G′B′ Values		
	R	G	B	R′	G′	B′
10% Gray	0.10000	0.10000	0.10000	0.29094	0.29094	0.29094
Red	0.49663	0.03315	0.05326	0.70307	0.13827	0.19467
Green	0.07300	0.34379	0.07297	0.23945	0.58072	0.23939
Blue	0.03129	0.05274	0.36063	0.13217	0.19340	0.59551

Table 7-B.   RGB linear signals and the R′G′B′ non-linear video signals for the four colors in the example.

Patch	Normalized XYZ Values			Absolute XYZ Values		
	X	Y	Z	X	Y	Z
10% Gray	0.09464	0.10000	0.10757	4.5428	4.8000	5.1636
Red	0.22485	0.13250	0.06340	10.7928	6.3600	3.0432
Green	0.16624	0.26731	0.11089	7.9795	12.8309	5.3227
Blue	0.09590	0.07012	0.34480	4.6032	3.3658	16.5504

Table 7-C.   Normalized and absolute XYZ values for the four colors in the example.

Patch	Absolute XYZ Values			DCDM X'Y'Z' Values		
	X	Y	Z	X'	Y'	Z'
10% Gray	4.5428	4.8000	5.1636	1599	1633	1680
Red	10.7928	6.3600	3.0432	2231	1820	1371
Green	7.9795	12.8309	5.3227	1986	2384	1700
Blue	4.6032	3.3658	16.5504	1607	1425	2629

Table 7-D.   Absolute XYZ values and DCDM X'Y'Z' values for the four colors in the example.

where the subscript abs represents the absolute values and the subscript norm represents the normalized values. Table 7-C gives the normalized and absolute XYZ values for these four patches assuming that the white is projected at a luminance of 48.00 cd/m^2 as recommended in SMPTE 431.1.

Using Equations the transfer function from Chapter 4 (equation 1-3), the DCDM X'Y'Z' values were calculated and are shown in Table 7-D. These DCDM X'Y'Z' values are the values that would be sent to the projector.

Assume the projector is a Reference Projector. Using Equations 4 – 6 the linear XYZ values were calculated from the DCDM X'Y'Z' code values in Table 5. Table 6 shows the DCDM X'Y'Z' code values and the linear XYZ values in the projector. The XYZ values in Table 7-E do not precisely match the XYZ values in Table 7-D because in the encoding step there is a rounding operation and in the decoding operation these rounded values are converted to XYZ values.

By the use of the inverse of Equation 32

$$\begin{pmatrix} X_{norm} \\ Y_{norm} \\ Z_{norm} \end{pmatrix} = \left(\frac{1}{48.00} \right) \times \begin{pmatrix} X_{abs} \\ Y_{abs} \\ Z_{abs} \end{pmatrix}$$

(33)

Patch	DCDM X'Y'Z' Values			Absolute XYZ Values		
	X'	Y'	Z'	X	Y	Z
10% Gray	1599	1633	1680	4.5418	4.7972	5.1645
Red	2231	1820	1371	10.7975	6.3593	3.0445
Green	1986	2384	1700	7.9794	12.8298	5.3259
Blue	1607	1425	2629	4.6011	3.3662	16.5454

Table 7-E. DCDM X'Y'Z' values and the absolute XYZ values for the four colors in the example at the Reference Projector.

Patch	Absolute XYZ Values			Normalized RGB Values		
	X	Y	Z	R	G	B
10% Gray	4.5418	4.7972	5.1645	0.10878	0.09607	0.11360
Red	10.7975	6.3593	3.0445	0.45028	0.04643	0.06750
Green	7.9794	12.8298	5.3259	0.13212	0.32197	0.10559
Blue	4.601	3.3662	16.5454	0.03813	0.05008	0.37729

Table 7-F. Absolute XYZ and normalized RGB values at the Reference Projector values for the four colors in the example

and then Equation 27, the normalized, linear RGB values in the Reference Projector were calculated from the absolute XYZ values. Table 7-F shows the result of these calculations.

How these normalized, linear RGB values are used inside any particular digital projector will be dependent on how the projector is made and will most likely vary from projector manufacturer to projector manufacturer. Therefore, the conversion of the normalized RGB values inside the projector is projector specific and is not shown here.

So, how does one implement this color space conversion? Do color correctors need to be rebuilt to work in XYZ rather than RGB? The answer to this second question is a strong no. The conversion from an R'G'B' working space to X'Y'Z' should be performed at the output of the color corrector or in a secondary processing step. If the digital master is assembled in a computer file system, than the color conversion can easily be applied in a batch processing step using software tools such as Apple's Shake™. If it is a 2K master, then real-time hardware color LUT boxes can be programmed to do the color space conversion from R'G'B' to X'Y'Z'. At the time of this writing, several color corrector manufacturers are planning to add the X'Y'Z' color conversion as an output option.

Color Metadata

Color metadata should be included with the Digital Cinema Distribution Master to identify the characteristics of the Reference Projector used in the creation of the master. These colorimetric characteristics include the calibrated red, green and blue primaries, the white point luminance and chromaticity and the measured contrast range of the projector in the mastering environment. Although $X'Y'Z'$ is explicitly defined as the color encoding of the displayed picture, this metadata helps the cinema projector determine if any gamut mapping is required.

In order to determine if the DCDM content is out-of-gamut, the projector need simply compute the R,G,B code value outputs of the color conversion matrix with the three red, green and blue primary inputs, and check to see if any of the resulting signals are out of range (greater than one or less than zero).

8

Color Processing in the Projector

The color processing in the projector provides several functions. The first is a means to calibrate the projector so that the image on the screen matches the Reference Projector primaries, white point and peak white luminance. This calibration compensates for differences in the spectral characteristics of optical components in the projector, including the lamp, reflectors, prism and projection optics. It also compensates for environmental characteristics like discolorations introduced by the portal glass or the screen itself.

This calibration is performed by measuring the luminance and chromaticity coordinates of an internally generated white field test pattern, along with the chromaticity coordinates of red, green and blue field test patterns. From these measured parameters that represent the uncorrected projector in its display environment, a linear matrix can be computed that converts the white point and primaries to the standard coordinates for the Reference Projector. Once this matrix has been computed and loaded, it is a good practice to verify that the calibrated projector is hitting the target coordinates, by repeating the measurements of the same test patterns.

The second color processing operation that is performed by the projector is to convert from the X′Y′Z′ input signal of the DCDM into the RGB (linear) signal that drives the modulators. This operation requires a linearization step, implemented with a gamma 2.6 transfer function as

119

described in Chapter 4, and is followed by a 3x3 matrix in linear space that converts from XYZ to the device—specific RGB signals. For a calibrated projector that matches the Reference Projector, this is an inverse of the color matrix used to convert from RGB to XYZ in the color encoding of the DCDM. In the DLP Cinema® projectors, the two linear matrices are combined into a single matrix that converts from XYZ to the calibrated primaries and white point of the Reference Projector.

This is all the processing that is required for the calibrated display of a X′Y′Z′ DCDM signal. However, most projectors will be capable of displaying other input formats, including 4:2:2 YC_bC_r input over a single SMPTE 292 serial digital interface. For this case, which applies to legacy MPEG2 digital cinema distribution masters as well as to most alternative content delivered live or taped via MPEG2 file format, it is necessary for the projector to also provide an input color space conversion matrix that converts from 4:2:2 YC_bC_r to fully-sampled R, G and B signals for display. This color matrix is the one described in ITU Rec. 709 for HDTV, and is applied to non-linear gamma-encoded signals. In most cases, this will also require a scaling of the incoming luminance signal from video code values (64 to 940 for 10 bits) to the full range code values internal to the projector (0 to 4096 for 12 bits). If the incoming signal covers the full range (0 to 1024), then this signal is accommodated by applying a unity gain.

In the JPEG2000 compression algorithm specified by DCI, the independent color channels are de-correlated by applying an Irreversible Color Transform, or ICT. This allows the total encoded bit-rate to be reduced substantially at equivalent peak signal to noise ratio (PSNR). The ICT specified within the JPEG2000 standard[1] is based on the ITU Rec. 601 matrix to convert from R′G′B′ to $Y′C′_bC′_r$, as shown in equation 1. Note that this matrix is applied to the non-linear, gamma-corrected signals. However, tests have shown that this same matrix can be used to transform the X′Y′Z′ DCDM signals into a $Y′C′_xC′_z$ that is substantially de-correlated. Although this is not fully optimized, it does allow the total encoded bit-rate to be reduced by a factor of two, while still being fully compatible with the JPEG2000 standard and the chip sets that support it.

$$\begin{pmatrix} Y′ \\ C′_b \\ C′_r \end{pmatrix} = \begin{pmatrix} 0.299 & 0.587 & 0.114 \\ -0.168736 & -0.331264 & 0.5 \\ 0.5 & -0.418688 & -0.081312 \end{pmatrix} \times \begin{pmatrix} R′ \\ G′ \\ B′ \end{pmatrix} \tag{1}$$

Since the DCI specification supports the input of two 4:2:2 sampled $Y′C′_xC′_z$ serial digital streams for the case of 48 FPS or stereo 24 FPS streams for 3D display, it is necessary to define a transform for converting from 4:2:2 $Y′C′_xC′_z$ to X′Y′Z′. The simplest way to do so is to use the standard

---

1. David S. Taubman and Michael W. Marcellin, *JPEG2000 Image Compression Fundamentals, Standards and Practice*, Kluwer Academic Publishers, © 2002, p. 421.

ICT matrix in the JPEG2000 encoder, but to turn off the Inverse ICT on playback, so that de-compressed the signal remains in Y'C'$_x$C'$_z$ color space. The Inverse ICT is specified in the JPEG2000 standard[2] as shown in equation 2.

$$\begin{pmatrix} R' \\ G' \\ B' \end{pmatrix} = \begin{pmatrix} 1 & 0 & 1.402 \\ 1 & -0.344136 & -0.714136 \\ 1 & 1.772 & 0 \end{pmatrix} \times \begin{pmatrix} Y' \\ C'_b \\ C'_r \end{pmatrix} \tag{2}$$

It should be noted that, at the time of this writing, the signal format and color transforms for stereo (3D) are not explicitly specified by the DCI System Specification v1.0, and have yet to be addressed by SMPTE DC28.

Gamut Mapping

In selecting X'Y'Z' color encoding for DCDM distribution, the DCI and SMPTE groups wanted to ensure that the color encoding standard supported not only today's Xenon-based digital cinema projectors, but that it could also be extended to support wider-gamut projectors in the future, perhaps those using a laser light source. Once a wider gamut projector is available, it could be used to create a DCDM that contains colors outside of the gamut of today's digital cinema projectors. So, the challenge is backward-compatibility. The display of wider gamut masters on a smaller gamut display requires some method of gamut mapping.

One approach to gamut mapping will be illustrated using an example of a film color that is outside of the gamut of today's digital cinema projectors. In Chapter 3, it was shown that there are some film colors that fall outside what a digital projector can produce. One of those colors, a cyan color shown in Figure 1, will be carried through the same calculations as above. For this exercise, the cyan color was defined by a set of Cineon code values, written to intermediate film, printed to print film, projected using a film projector, and the colorimetry of the color was measured off the screen. Therefore, while it represents a computer generated color, and not one that was captured by a camera negative film, this is a color that has been produced on a color print film, not a theoretical color. Table 8-A summarizes the calculations for this cyan color through the system.

Table 8-A shows that the Reference Projector normalized R value, R$_{RP}$, is negative. This means the Reference Projector cannot produce this color because the limit on what colors the Reference Projector can produce is the set of colors in which the normalized RGB values are all

---

2. Ibid. p. 422.

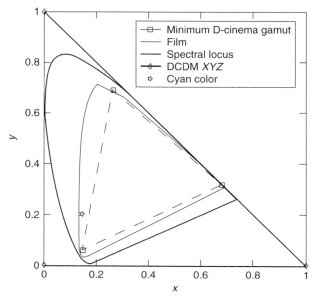

Figure 8-1.   The Cyan Color Compared to the Film and Reference Projector Color Gamuts.

Color Representation	Values		
Film *XYZ*	2.799	3.822	12.303
Film *xyz*	0.1479	0.2020	0.6501
DCDM *X′Y′Z′* Values	1327	1496	2346
Reference Projector Absolute *XYZ* Values	2.797	3.820	12.305
Reference Projector Normalized RGB Values, R_{RP}, G_{RP}, B_{RP}	−0.035	0.094	0.278
Gamut Mapping by Clipping, RGB Values, R_{RP}, G_{RP}, B_{RP}	0.000	0.094	0.278
Gamut Mapping by Clipping, *XYZ* Values	3.546	4.172	12.305
Gamut Mapping by Clipping, *xyz* Values	0.1770	0.2084	0.6145

Table 8-A.   Following a cyan color through the D-Cinema encoding.

greater than or equal to 0 and less than or equal to 1. This result is expected because Figure 1 shows that this cyan color is inside the film gamut, but outside the Reference Projector gamut.

Because R_{RP} in the Reference Projector is negative, the Reference Projector cannot produce this color and must produce some other color. This reproduction of an out of gamut color within the gamut of the display device is known as Gamut Mapping. All image display systems must have some gamut mapping strategy. Even film has a gamut mapping strategy, but because it is done in chemistry, it is not as obvious as the gamut mapping in a digital system. Neither DCI nor SMPTE defines a gamut mapping strategy for digital cinema. That is a decision that will be made by manufacturers of digital cinema projectors. There are many references in published literature that describe a large number of gamut mapping strategies implemented in other applications. However, a few comments can be made about different strategies and about how the information in the DCDM file can be used to implement a gamut mapping strategy.

In this example, the simplest and easiest gamut mapping strategy is to clip all Reference Projector Normalized RGB Values less than zero to zero and all Reference Projector Normalized RGB Values greater than one to one. The problem with this simple clip strategy is that it usually leads to hue shifts in the color produced on the screen and observers are quite sensitive to hue shifts. If a color goes a little darker or lighter or it goes a little less saturated (gamut mapping usually does not make a color go more saturated), the color change is usually less objectionable than if the color changes hue. Certainly there are some hue shifts that are acceptable, but in general designers try to avoid anything more than a small hue shift. So a simple clipping of the code values is usually not a preferred gamut mapping strategy. Table A and Figure 8.2 show the effect of clipping of the cyan color discussed above.

Figure 8.2 has been greatly expanded in the region near the cyan color so that the shift in chromaticity due to the clipping can more easily be seen. The clipped cyan color lies on a line connecting the chromaticity coordinates of the original cyan color and the Reference Projector red primary. This line is shown as the dotted line on Figure 8.2.

Another problem with the simple clip strategy for gamut mapping can be seen in Figure 8.2. There are a number of possible colors lying on the line connecting the original cyan color and the gamut mapped cyan color that would all be gamut mapped to the same cyan color. In an image, the result is that a series of colors that vary slightly, as in a saturation series, will be mapped to the same color. In the image, this will look like a uniform blob of color, creating a contouring artifact that is not natural.

Therefore, another gamut mapping strategy is to map the color that is farthest from the gamut boundary to the gamut boundary and colors that are between the farthest color and the gamut boundary to colors slightly inside the gamut boundary. This gives a compressed saturation scale to the mapped colors, but at least there is some discrimination among the colors and the end result is more pleasing. Figure 8.3 shows a possible gamut mapping strategy that implements this approach. In Figure 8.2 the original cyan color is 0.030 chromaticity coordinate units away from the gamut boundary. Assume this was the cyan color that was farthest from the gamut boundary. Then in Figure 8.3, the actual cyan color was moved 0.030 xy units to put it right on the boundary. In addition, a color that was 0.020 xy units outside the boundary was moved 0.0225 xy units, so it

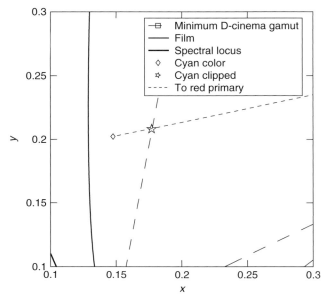

Figure 8-2. Clipping the cyan color code values in the Reference Projector.

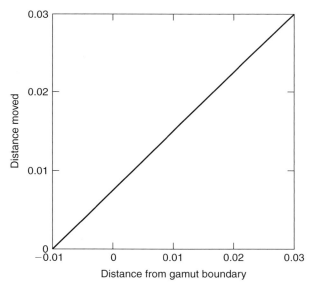

Figure 8-3. A Gamut Mapping Strategy to Preserve Color Discrimination.

will fall 0.0025 xy units inside the boundary. A color that was originally right on the gamut boundary was moved 0.0075 xy units. In all cases in this example, the movement is toward the red primary. Finally, any color more than 0.010 xy units inside the boundary will not be moved at all.

This strategy to move colors, even some that are inside the gamut boundary so that not all colors fall at the same point, can be applied to all possible hue angles. It is more common to move the colors toward the neutral axis (the white point chromaticity coordinates) than toward the chromaticity coordinates of a primary, but the principle is the same. In defining this strategy it is useful to know how far out of gamut any color might be. In particular, it is most helpful if the color that is the greatest distance from the gamut boundary is known. For example, if the maximum distance of the cyan original from the gamut boundary had been 0.060 xy units instead of 0.030 xy units, Figure 8.3 would have been drawn a bit differently. In this case, possibly even colors as far as 0.020 inside the gamut boundary would have been moved. The point is that as original colors fall farther from the gamut boundary, more colors inside the gamut will be moved. If no colors fall outside the gamut boundary, then no colors need to be moved. Therefore, it would be useful to know the limits of the colors that may fall outside the gamut of the projector that is displaying the images.

In this example, the cyan color was referred to as the original color, but it is really the color that was encoded in the DCDM file. So the original color really means the color that is desired and that the digital projector should make. But in the case in which the gamut of the display system during the mastering of the production is larger than the gamut of the display system in the theater, the digital projector in the theater has to gamut map some of the colors in order to display them.

In order to know how far to move the colors, both the colors outside and inside the digital projector gamut, it would be useful to have some estimate of the maximum distance any color could be outside the digital projector gamut. One estimate is that the maximum distance is defined by the XYZ primaries used in the encoding of the DCDM. However, this is an extreme case and in practice gives little useful information. It would also be possible to compute the digital projector RGB values from the DCDM X'Y'Z' values for every pixel in the production and find the one pixel that is the greatest distance outside the gamut boundary. However, this will be a very time-consuming calculation and is not practical.

If, however, the chromaticity coordinates of the mastering projector primaries were known, it would be relatively easy to compare those chromaticity coordinates to the chromaticity coordinates of the primaries of the digital projector in the theatre. If the mastering projector primaries are on or inside the gamut of the theater digital projector, no gamut mapping strategy is needed. If however, the chromaticity coordinates of the mastering projector primaries are far outside the gamut of the theater projector, a considerable amount of gamut mapping may be needed. Thus even the knowledge of the location of the mastering projector primaries can help greatly in the definition of the gamut mapping strategy. This is why the SMPTE standard for the DCDM includes metadata that specifies the color primaries of the mastering projector. This does not mean that all digital cinema projectors have to use this color metadata, but for those that do, there is the possibility of displaying the images more closely to the creative intent as defined by what was seen in the mastering suite.

Tone Mapping

In Chapter 4, the transfer function was described as a representation of the luminance level above theatre black, or a relative luminance encoding. Some people have suggested that there is a benefit to be gained by encoding luminance in absolute terms, so that tone mapping could be performed by the cinema projector reproducing the image.

Current practice in digital cinema is to master on a high contrast projector, and assign the lowest code value of luminance to the lowest luminance available to the projector. If we are in 12 bit space, valid code values from 0 to 4095 and operating with a 1800:1 contrast projector, the projector's black will have code value 0, which will correspond to luminance of 1/1800 of peak white on the screen.

Consider the following plot of transfer functions shown in Figure 8.4. The plot is for 0 to 4095 gamma 2.6 encoded DCDM equivalent on the abscissa (10 to 1000 displayed), luminance output as a 16 bit linear number from 0 to 65535 on the ordinate. (10 to 10,000 displayed).

The magenta curve is the "natural" luminance function of a projector with 1800:1 contrast ratio. This is how the image would appear if the projector were given an unprocessed signal.

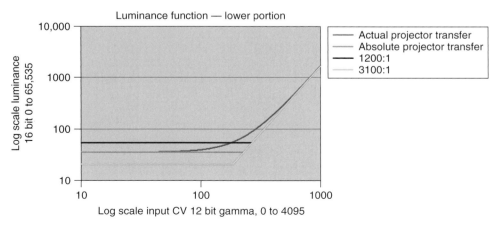

Figure 8-4. Transfer functions for projectors with different contrast ratios.

The blue curve represents the projector transfer function where the projector knows that it is to "do its best" to show information at the prescribed luminance, until it reaches its native black level, where it will clip. This curve shown is for a projector of 1200:1

The cyan curve represents the performance of the 1800:1 mastering projector with a calculated response to the absolute luminance function. It should be noted that to go from the natural response (magenta curve) to the absolute response (cyan curve) requires a very high gain calculation at the lowest code values.

The yellow curve is the response of a 3100:1 projector, with a calculated response to the absolute luminance. The actual image displayed on this projector would be clipped at the black level of the mastering projector. (Not shown is a curve representing the natural response of a 3100:1 projector showing the image mastered for a 1800:1)

It is important to note that employing an absolute response system means that code values below the minimum response of the projector in question are clipped for projectors of lower contrast ratio than the mastering projector, and for higher contrast ratio, the master must provide information to the projector about the minimum valid code value in the image.

The alternative of absolute luminance encoding would calculate the actual luminance on screen in mastering, and map it to a system where code value 0 is "absolute black". In practice this would place 1/2000 contrast ratio black at code value 210 (12 bit gamma). The master would then reflect true and absolute luminance in the Y value. When this information is received by the projector in the theatre, it would interpret the incoming code values and "do its best" to reflect the correct absolute luminance in the projected image. Code values below the blackest black possible from the mastering projector would be mapped to black.

If the theatre projector is of higher contrast, the projector would respect the black level of the mastering projector, and never go darker than the mastering projector did. On the other hand, if the projector has lower contrast than the mastering projector, the projector would display the proper luminance on the screen down to the point where it is incapable of going darker. At that point it would clip. There is a possibility that the projector could be smarter and do some tone mapping and alter the transfer function in some (global) way to make the dark part of the image look better.

Practical tests were performed by the SMPTE DC28 Color Ad Hoc group to test the image quality implications of absolute black coding, and the requirements of theatre and mastering projectors to manage this. Several minutes of motion picture clips with deep shadow detail were optimally mastered on a projector with a measured contrast ratio of 1800:1. This was used as the source material to evaluate the several schemes. The clips selected made good use of rich blacks.

The first approach was to display "true" luminance where possible with no tone mapping. The reference pictures were mastered at 1800:1 and displayed at 1800:1 while passing through a transformation where 0 equals absolute black. This was done by creating a custom LUT to emulate the entire process of compensating for elevated black level in the mastering data, and reintroducing the elevated black level in the display projector. This emulation was performed to map the input data using a single LUT, which reflected the entire processing chain, including quantization to 12 bits for distribution. The resulting transfer function was essentially a unity transformation, where the input and output values differed by round off amounts of 0 or ±1.

The same master was also displayed at a contrast ratio of 1200:1. A LUT was developed which emulated the process to provide absolute luminance on the lower contrast projector. The resulting transfer function followed the mastering luminance (on screen) exactly to the limit of the projector's capability. Lower levels were clipped.

The same master was also displayed at a contrast ratio of 3100:1. A projector was modified to achieve a contrast ratio of 3100:1. The 1800:1 master was displayed at 3100:1, where the projector transfer function clipped at 1800:1 (in other words, no use was made of the extra contrast).

The pictures were examined closely at the three different projection contrast ratios. There was no apparent impairment when comparing the original 1800:1 master to the master that was processed up and down to 1800:1. As mentioned above, the comparison of LUTs revealed 1 count differences in code values—not surprisingly, there was no visual significance to these values. It was expected that there would be some image impairment due to the high gain required in the internal transfer function LUT to create the "absolute" response of the projector.

The display at 1200:1 contrast ratio revealed some difficulties. Information which was available in the 1800:1 system was not visible at 1200:1. In a number of scenes, this was a significant loss of information, resulting in some large areas of blocked blacks. Some of these blocked areas were large enough to appear milky. From a mathematical point of view, to create the corrected LUT to back out the projector black luminance requires a very high gain at the bottom end, with resulting potential to exaggerate noise at that level.

The 3100:1 display looked identical to the 1800:1 display, because the blacks were lifted to a level to equal the level of the 1800:1 master.

A second test was designed to look at the image quality where mastering projector black is equal to 0 and the images were displayed on 1200:1 and 3100:1 projectors with each projector mapping this code value to its darkest black.

This is called "nature's tone mapping" because it provides a gentle curve at the lowest end of the tone scale, which maps all input code values to a luminance value on the projector. The range displayed is "true" for the top roughly 99% of tone scale, but compresses in the bottom 1% (or expands in the case of the higher contrast projector). Any code value change in the master provides an absolute luminance change in the exhibition projector, although it may be compressed compared to the master. This compression is naturally performed by the fact that a fixed amount of light is being added to the entire image. This amount of light adds significant luminance only at the bottom 1% of the tone scale.

For the 1200:1 contrast projector, the mastered image where 0 equals best projector black was played on the low contrast projector. A standard 2.6 gamma function was utilized. The resulting image showed modulation for each code value in the master, resulting in a soft toe to the tone curve. The visual result was pleasing because it maintained details which were in the original, although with lower dynamics.

On the 3100:1 contrast projector, the mastered image was allowed to go darker than was seen in the mastering suite. Intermediate tones were examined for any unwanted color shading, but no artifacts were seen. The deeper blacks looked better, shots which previously had been milky showed better dynamics and looked cleaner. The improved contrast improved the look of all shots in the test clips.

To observe the differences in image presentation between "absolute" and "projector" black, we toggled between approaches on still frames and during motion sequences.

In the 1200:1 displayed contrast case, the "absolute" clipped toe transfer function to display absolute luminance hid detail that was for the most part desirable. There were large areas of clipped black with no detail or texture. These tended to look milky. There were a small minority of shots that looked slightly better with black clipped (this would be around 2% of shots, with small areas of irrelevant texture near black). The "projector black" (smooth toe) transfer function maintained details and textures, at the expense of slightly lower contrast in the darkest areas. The tone mapping provided by the projector's natural transfer function provided satisfying detail and texture in the dark areas, and most shots appeared to have improved contrast as a result. In comparing the two approaches, there was a strong overall preference to the smooth tone map provided by nature.

In the 3100:1 displayed contrast case, the clipped transfer function provided a slightly milky image that looked just like the 1800:1 mastered image. When the transfer function was opened up to allow the entire range, the image looked substantially better. The blacks got deeper, and information was preserved—in fact, enhanced—near black. Once again, the smooth toe transfer function provided a remarkably improved image.

For taking the master to higher or to lower contrast displays, a smooth tone map is preferred to a clipped tone map. Displaying absolute luminance provided noticeable impairment to the appearance of the image in both cases.

9

DLP Cinema® Case Study

DLP Cinema® projection technology was developed by Texas Instruments, incorporating feedback from extensive demonstrations and testing with industry experts that began in 1997. This chapter describes how DLP Cinema® technology works and provides a case study of how the engineers at Texas Instruments adapted and extended their technology to meet the needs of the motion picture industry. DLP Cinema® projectors are now available from TI's three licensed manufacturers, Barco, Christie and NEC.

The light modulator in DLP Cinema® projectors is a digital micro-mirror device (DMD), with today's 2K devices having a display resolution of 2048H × 1080V. The DMD is an electro-mechanical device that contains over two million individually addressable mirrors that operate in a bi-stable mode, switching light on and off at each pixel. Each individual pixel is controlled using underlying conventional 5-volt CMOS circuitry. The deflection circuitry, hinges and mirrors are built on the CMOS circuitry using conventional semiconductor processes. The bi-stable function provides for fast and precise rotation of each micro-mirror through angles of +12 and −12 degrees. The structure of two micro-mirrors is shown in Figure 9.1.

The optical switching action of the mirrors is illustrated in Figure 9.2. When the mirror rotates to its "on" state (+12 degrees), light from the illumination system is directed into the pupil of the projection lens, and a bright pixel is projected onto the screen. When the mirror rotates to its "off" state (−12 degrees), light is directed outside of the pupil of the projection lens to a light absorber and a projected pixel appears dark. The bi-stable switching of light into or out of the

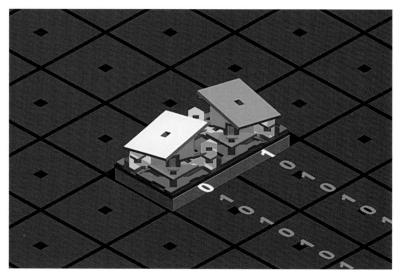

Figure 9-1. DMD structure illustrated for 2 mirrors.

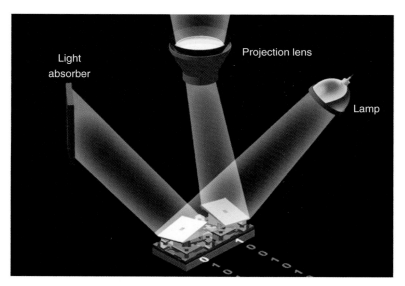

Figure 9-2. Optical Switching characteristics of DMD elements.

pupil of the projection lens is used to produce grayscale images by modulating the light temporally, using pulse width modulation (PWM). The native transfer function of the DMD device itself is linear, from input signal to light output. More than any other modulation device, the DMD imaging system is truly digital.

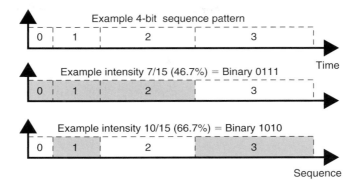

In the binary PWM case, the least significant bit (LSB), bit 0,
consumes $1/(2^n - 1)$ of the total frame

Figure 9-3. A simple example of Pulse Width Modulation (PWM).

Pulse width modulation produces a grayscale image by assigning each bit plane of video data to a portion of the frame time. Figure 9.3 shows how the frame time can be divided into bit planes. This figure gives two examples of how individual bit planes might be turned on (as shaded) to create two different intensity levels. To keep this example simple, only 4 bit signals are shown. In this simple case, the least significant bit (LSB), bit 0, controls $1/(2^n - 1)$ or 1/15th of the total frame time. Bit 1 controls twice the LSB time, bit 2 controls four times the LSB time, and bit 3 control eight times the LSB time. The duration of a given bit is defined by the following equation, where F is the input source frame rate (Hz), n is the number of occurrences of bit b during the frame period and B is the total number of bits:

$$\tau_b = \frac{2^b}{F \times n \times (2^B - 1)}$$

In DLP Cinema® projectors, the input bit planes are refreshed four times for the 24 Hz input, producing an effective refresh rate of 96 Hz, which eliminates flicker.

TI first brought a prototype DLP projector to Hollywood in 1997 for a demonstration at Paramount Studios. In order to minimize the impact on cinema installations, the projector head was designed to mount on a conventional film lamp house, with the DLP Cinema® projection head taking the place of the mechanical film projector head. To keep the light path in line with the output light path of a traditional film projector, the light path utilized fold mirrors. A photograph of this prototype projector is shown in Figure 9.4. This projector employed three SXGA (1280H × 1024V) digital mirror devices, using a Total Internal Reflection (TIR) prism to split the light into red, green and blue components. In order to maximize the projected resolution of the common

Figure 9-4. The prototype DLP Cinema® projector.

1.85 and 2.39 film projection formats, two horizontal anamorphic lenses were employed, one at 1.5:1 and the other at 1.9:1.

A variety of film clips were mastered for these demonstrations, and compared to film release prints by projecting in a split-screen. Studio experts, directors and cinematographers were invited to comment on their observations. Although most were surprised by the quality of the digital pictures, many were quick to point out deficiencies in contrast and color gamut compared to the film print. Many also found the visible pixels to be annoying, especially with the widescreen 2.39:1 picture which used the 1.9:1 anamorphic lens. TI listened to these comments and the engineers went back to work.

INDUSTRY FIRSTS

DLP Cinema® technology was introduced to the industry in a series of milestone demonstrations.

1997	First demonstrations in Hollywood
1999	George Lucas releases "Star Wars- Episode 1" to 3 DLP Cinema® screens
2000	First DLP Cinema® 1.3K product ships
2003	First DLP Cinema® 2K product ships
2005	First DLP Cinema® 3D release- Disney's "Chicken Little"

Table 9-A. Major Milestones in DLP Cinema®

Expanded Color Gamut

In order to widen the color gamut to more closely match that of color print film, a yellow dichroic notch filter was inserted in the optical path. Extensive samples were taken of real-world colors to establish a working reference, using a Photo Research PR-650 spectro-radiometer. This yellow notch filter expanded the color gamut from the ITU Rec. 709 color gamut used by standard DLP® projectors to a new set of red and green primaries that encompass the film gamut in the critical yellow region where many flesh tones fall. Of course, the light output is reduced by adding trim filters, so they must be used judiciously. For example, a cyan filter could also be used to encompass more of the deep film cyan colors, but only at the expense of significant light loss. Through practical tests with careful grading to match a projected film print, the new expanded DLP Cinema® color gamut was judged to be a significant improvement and sufficient to encompass all but the deepest cyan (aquamarine) colors. Over five years of practical experience with this color gamut led DCI to specify the DLP Cinema color primaries as the minimum color gamut for the Reference Projector (see Chapter 3) when they published their specifications in 2005.

Since the DMD device is inherently linear, it requires more bit depth than most other display technologies. This bit depth requirement can be estimated using contrast sensitivity functions such as the Barten model described in Chapter 4. The bit depth requirement is a function of light level and contrast range, as shown in Figure 9.5, with a range of luminances from 8 ft L (minimum theatrical) to 16 ft L (standard film open gate luminance) and 35 ft L (studio monitor). At 2000:1, the number of bits required for a cinema presentation at 14 ft L is between 14 and 15 bits. The bit depth of the DLP Cinema® projectors was increased from 14 to 16 bits to meet this requirement.

The initial projector prototype also used the non-linear transfer function specified in ITU-R Rec. 709 to reduce the number of bits required in the input signal. However, some contouring artifacts were still visible in 10-bit sources and calculations showed that a pure power law with a gamma of 2.5 could reduce the number of bits required to less than 10 bits (over a contrast range of 2000:1). This is illustrated in Figure 9.5. Furthermore, practical color grading tests showed that

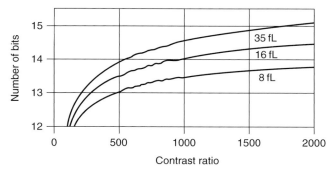

Figure 9-5. Number of bits required as a function of contrast ratio and luminance level.

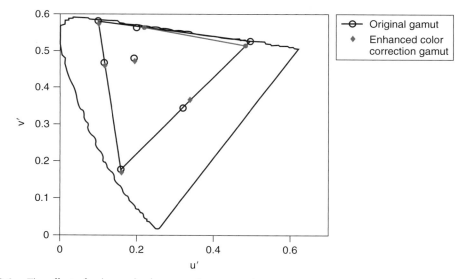

Figure 9-6. The effect of enhanced color correction processing.

the resulting pictures more closely matched the contrast of a projected film print, and that using a gamma of 2.6 provided the most effective (and quickest) working environment. As described in Chapter 4, the gamma 2.6 transfer function is also a good approximation for the contrast sensitivity profile of the human visual system as described by the Barten equation.

Practical color grading tests with the new expanded gamut also uncovered a problem with reproducing red hues consistently with film. The red primary had been moved to a longer wavelength to make it less orange in hue. However, constant hue lines in this region are highly non-linear. This is known as the Abney effect.[1] An enhanced color correction capability was developed to

---

1. Mark D. Fairchild, *Color Appearance Models*, Wiley ©. 2005, p.117–119.

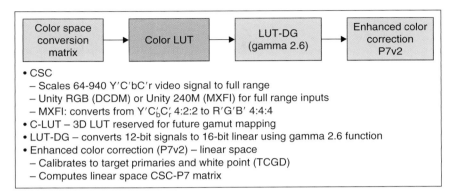

Figure 9-7.   DLP Cinema® Color Processing.

correct this problem by moving the red primary toward blue, thus moving onto a reddish hue line, as shown in Figure 9.6. This enhanced color correction capability provided for the calibration of not only the three projector primaries, but also the placement of three secondary colors (cyan, magenta and yellow), and the calibrated white point. TI dubbed this new capability "P7".

Color Processing

The DLP Cinema® color processing chain, as shown in Figure 9.7, was designed to support the evolving digital cinema standards as well as standard video and graphics inputs. The primary input signal for digital cinema is a 1080 line by 2048 pixels per line, 24 frames per second progressive digital signal delivered over dual SMPTE 292 HD-SDI links. This dual-link implementation, formalized in SMPTE 372, supports 10 or 12 bit data in either 4:2:2 or 4:4:4 data sampling formats.

The front-end of the process involves non-linear, gamma-corrected signals that have a 12-bit data path. This includes all functions up to lookup table 2 (LUT2). LUT2 converts the gamma-corrected signal to linear display data and outputs 16 bit data. The remaining linear signal processing has 16-bit resolution.

If the incoming signal is sub-sampled 4:2:2 data, it is first converted to fully sampled 4:4:4 data. The color space converter (CSC1) is a matrix used to convert from YC_bC_r to RGB or from YC_xC_z to XYZ, allowing the system to support both the original HDTV-based signal format as well as the XYZ digital cinema standard. Provision is provided for adjusting the offset and gain of the incoming signal to accommodate the standard video signal range of 64 to 940 (10 bit ITU Rec. 709), or a full range signal of 0 to 1024 (10 bits).

A two-dimensional resizer provides horizontal and vertical scaling using polyphase FIR filters, optimized to avoid ringing and thus avoiding the traditional edginess associated with video signals.

A 3D-LUT provides gamut-mapping capabilities as described in Chapter 8 but is not currently used for D-Cinema applications. 12-bit signal precision is maintained from input to output with support for multiple lattice sizes up to $64 \times 64 \times 64$. LUT2 converts the gamma-corrected signal to a linear 16-bit signal, using a simple power law function with a gamma of 2.6.

The final enhanced color correction block is a color space conversion implemented in linear light space with 16 bits of precision. This is the "CSC-P7" processing block that was described earlier. It also provides a calibration function, which takes on-site measurements of the screen chromaticities of red, green, blue and white test patterns (measured color gamut data) and, comparing them to the target color gamut data, computes a compensating color matrix. This effectively corrects for not only the projector's native color characteristics, but also for the color characteristics of the screen, port glass and the Xenon lamp itself. This compensates for any projector or site-specific characteristics, making it possible to lock down the rest of the color processing operations.

This enhanced color correction block is also used to implement the color space conversion from XYZ data to the projector's calibrated RGB primaries and white point. As specified by DCI and SMPTE RP 431.2 on Reference Projector, the incoming channels are normalized to 3794 X', 3960 Y' and 3890 Z' and the output gains set so that this produces a peak white of 48 cd/m^2. This means that code values above this white point are clipped in the process, but this extra range could be used if the industry decides to shift the white point to something other than 0.314x, 0.315y (as was described in Chapter 4), while still providing for a peak white luminance of 48 cd/m^2.

CREATIVE USES OF THE 3D LUT

The 3D color look-up table has also been used for other functions in post production. Some facilities providing digital intermediate services generate a 3D LUT that emulates the characteristics of color print film, with this LUT generated from closed loop calibration of their output film recording and photochemical processing. This 3D LUT can be loaded into the reference projector that is used in mastering, so that color corrections made in the mastering suite appear exactly as they will on the projected film print that is produced at the end of the process. For the film release, the color corrected printing density data is simply sent to the film recorders. As described in Chapter 6, for D-cinema release the film print LUT must be rendered into the data before output to the DCDM files.

Another innovative use of the 3D LUT capability was described by Visual Effects Supervisor Rob Legato in an article in Millimeter magazine.[2] For "The Aviator", Martin Scorsese wanted to make this period movie set in the 1930's through 1950's look like the original 2-color and 3-color Technicolor prints that were available at the time. Josh Pines of Technicolor characterized the color of these original Technicolor prints and built custom 3D color LUTs that emulated these characteristics, so that the color grading process could be streamlined. When the digital intermediate process was completed, these custom LUTs were rendered into the final color corrected data before output to film and digital files.

White Point

The white point used in the first DLP demonstrations in Hollywood was D65, compatible with video mastering practices. However, the film projection standard (SMPTE 196M) defines the open gate chromaticity as 5400 K. So the first suggestion was to calibrate the DLP Cinema® projectors to a 5400 K white point. This was tried, but side by side demonstrations with film projectors uncovered inconsistencies. Two things became clear: the white point of film projectors varies a lot, and the average white point was very different from the industry standard. Figure 9.8 shows a plot of measured screen chromaticities from an industry survey.

This raised several questions. What causes this variability? And why is the average white point so different from industry standards? And does it even matter? Although all the projectors had

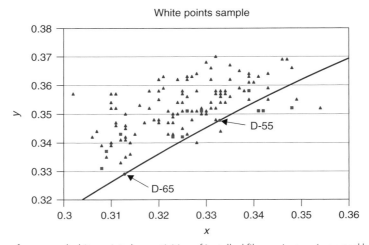

Figure 9-8. Survey of measured white point chromaticities of installed film projectors (reported by M. Cowan, 2002).

2. Michael Goldman, "Seeking Vintage Color", Millimeter, December 2004.

Xenon light sources, and the spectral output of Xenon lamps does not vary that much, variations are introduced by the coatings on the reflectors, the heat mirror, as well as the lens, port glass and the screen itself. With traditional film projectors, there is no means of compensating for these variations short of using color correction gels, and trading off some light. This is sometimes done with critical color timing rooms in the film laboratories.

The second question is more complicated and requires a historical perspective. Originally, film projectors used carbon arc light sources whose native color temperature was 5400 K, so this was established as the standard. Xenon lamps were introduced in the 1960s and rapidly displaced carbon arc lamps due to higher light output and less labor. The carbon rods burned down and had to be replaced after each show. The standard remained at 5400 K for backward compatibility. However, the most efficient white point for Xenon lamps was actually much cooler and greener than 5400 K. Over time, manufacturers of projectors adjusted their reflector coatings to maximize efficiency, providing higher lumens with lower wattage lamps.

And finally, does it even matter? Research has shown that the human observer adapts quickly and completely to a wide range of color temperatures, particularly if pictures are viewed in a darkened theatre. In nature, we have learned to accommodate to the wide range of color temperatures from dawn to dusk, and in the modern world to a wide variety of artificial lighting. So, in practice, the wide range of measured chromaticities in Figure 9.8 never created customer complaints, because it is well within the range of white point adaptation. Therefore it is not really a problem.

So, that still left the question as to what the white point should be for digital cinema. The variability in optical coatings, port glass and screens can be easily corrected with digital calibration. Texas Instruments picked a white point of $0.314x$, $0.351y$ for two reasons. It was an efficient operating point for the Xenon lamps used in both film and digital projectors. And secondly, it was in the center of the scatter plot representing current practice with traditional film projectors. Finally, tests were conducted to verify that it is a practical working white point for critical side by side tests with film. Over the last several years, this white point has been used for the commercial mastering and exhibition of over 300 movies. This white point was adopted by DCI and became the basis for the SMPTE Standard for Screen Luminance, Chrominance and Uniformity, SMPTE 431.1.

2000:1 Contrast

In addition to the improvements in color gamut and calibration, another major performance improvement was nearly doubling the sequential contrast from approximately 1200:1 to 2000:1. This enabled DLP Cinema® projectors to produce deep, rich blacks that match the typical blacks on a projected film print. This improvement in contrast that was delivered with the DC2K DMDs made a huge difference in picture quality allowing darker film-like blacks to be reproduced and boosting the sensation of sharpness[3]. In fact, it could be argued that the contrast improvement was probably more important to improving the picture quality than doubling the spatial resolution of the DMD.

This contrast improvement was accomplished by a combination of incremental improvements to the DMD devices. The first step was the so-called "black" chip. An anodized black substrate coating minimized back-reflection between the active mirrors on the DMD, thereby improving contrast. The second step was to reduce the gap between mirrors. And the final step was to increase the deflection angle to dump the off-state light further outside of the collection pupil of the projection lens.

For mastering applications, the contrast can be further enhanced by adding an aperture to the projection lens, trading light for higher contrast. Typically, the sequential contrast of the picture can be increased by 20% or so with a tradeoff of 50% in lumen output, making it feasible to achieve contrast ratios of as high as 2400:1 in darkened mastering rooms. This is a good practice, as it is always best to do the critical color grading and quality control functions on the best (highest contrast) projector.

2K Resolution

To minimize the visibility of the mirror structure in projected images, Texas Instruments developed a new DMD device, the DC2K, expanding the mirrored array to 1080 lines by 2048 (2K) pixels. This also eliminated the need for an anamorphic lens for the "flat" 1.85 format. The DC2K DMDs also substantially increased the MTF of the projected picture compared to the previous SXGA DMDs, as shown in Figure 9.9, producing sharper, cleaner pictures.

For comparison, the MTF of a typical film answer print and release print is also shown, based on the study commissioned by ITU-R Study Group 6 in 2001.[4] The film MTF response is measured by scanning the print stocks with a microdensitometer, so this does not include the additional losses in projecting a film print due to unsteadiness or thermal effects in the gate. In summary, although the MTF of the original projectors with the 1.2K DMDs was a good match for an ideal film release print, one can see that the 2K projector has higher MTF through much of the range than a first-generation film answer print.

---

3. R.W.G. Hunt, *The Reproduction of Color*, 6th Edition, Wiley, © 2004, p. 329.
4. ITU-R Study Group 6, "MTF Analysis of Film System", 2003.

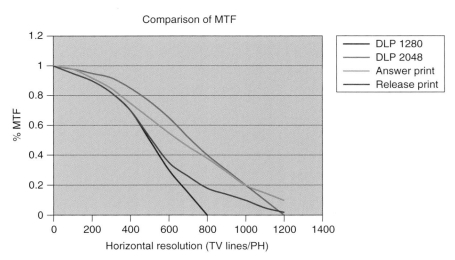

Figure 9-9. Modulation Transfer Function (MTF) of DLP Projectors compared to Film Answer Print and Release Print.

Cinema Features

To meet the requirements of the cinema market, Texas Instruments also developed several new features that are now available on all DLP Cinema® projectors. These include Cinelink™ link encryption, Cinecanvas™ subtitles, an anamorphic lens for widescreen (2.39:1) presentation and keystone correction and digital aperture plate for geometry correction. Each of these will be described in more detail.

Cinelink™ link encryption prevents the unauthorized recording of unencrypted content as it is played back from the digital cinema server in the cinema, thereby thwarting piracy. TI's initial Cinelink™ implementation was proprietary, but as the DCI security requirements were communicated, this was replaced by Cinelink™ 2, a cryptographically secure link encryption using a 128 bit AES key.

Cinecanvas™ provides on-screen subtitles, taking the subtitle information from an XML file on the digital cinema server, generating the subtitles and superimposing them over the picture. Texas Instruments submitted its file format to SMPTE for standardization, and this is the basis of the SMPTE 429.5 Standard for Digital Cinema Packaging Subtitle Distribution Format. This file supports subtitles in either of two forms: timed text, or graphics in Portable Network Graphics (PNG) format.

Within the projector, an overlay function is provided for subtitling, supporting up to 2 planes of 8-bit graphics containing RGB plus alpha channels in PNG format. The full Porter-Duff compositing operators are supported along with fade and priority selection. In addition, timed-text inputs are supported, which are rendered to anti-aliased text characters in these overlay planes for real-time subtitle insertion.

Widescreen (2.39:1) presentation is supported by an optional anamorphic lens attachment that stretches the image horizontally by a factor of 1.26. The DCDM image structure for the 2:39 format calls for 2048 pixels by 858 vertical lines. Within the projector, the image is expanded digitally by the same factor, filling the 1080 lines of the DMD array. This approach makes senses for cinemas where the 1.85 and 2.39 formats are presented with common screen heights and variable side masking, in other words, where the 2.39:1 format is truly a wider screen. Although the anamorphic attachment has a small (few percent) transmission loss, this approach yields more than 20% more light than the alternative of just zooming the lens to adjust for the 25% increase in picture width.

The ideal placement of the projector is aligned with the center of the screen. Architectural constraints often make this impossible. Typically, projectors have a down-angle of 5 to 10% and in some cases are installed off-center as well. This produces an image distortion known as keystone distortion or keystoning. The best way to correct for keystone distortion is to use a telecentric lens whose mount accommodates mechanical lens shift. All DLP Cinema® projectors have this capability.

Traditional film projectors typically have no adjustment for keystoning, other than an aperture plate that can be filed for each installation to "square up" the corners. This minimizes objections, because it keeps the borders of the picture square, even though the projected picture is still distorted. DLP Cinema® projectors are also equipped with a "digital aperture plate" capability, so that the edges of the projected image can be trimmed to match the screen.

DLP Cinema® 3D

Texas Instruments was approached by James Cameron and other creative visionaries in 2003 and encouraged to develop a solution for projecting 3D pictures with a single projector. Although dual-projector solutions were commonplace in theme park installations, a single projector solution was deemed much more viable for general cinema exhibition. The DMD technology was certainly fast enough to support the higher frame rates required. Basically, the approach was to interleave two 24 FPS streams (left eye and right eye), and to replicate the interleaved stream by a factor of two, produced an aggregate frame rate of 96 FPS.

This single-projector 3D presentation capability was delivered in an Enhanced Formatter Interface Board (EFIB) in 2004, and publicly demonstrated on a big screen for the first time to a wide industry audience at ShoWest in March 2005. Several leading directors (George Lucas, James Cameron, Robert Zemeckis, Robert Rodriguez and Peter Jackson) provided clips and shared their enthusiasm for digital 3D presentation, and their plans for producing 3D movies. Many exhibitors in the audience were also excited about the opportunity this presented to market a spectacular new experience to their customers.

Digital 3D presentation, and the implications for post production and distribution, is covered in detail in Chapter 11.

10
Digital Display Technologies

In addition to DLP® technology, LCoS (liquid crystal on Silicon) technologies have been applied to large screen digital cinema presentation, including JVC's D-ILA™ (Digitally addressed Image Light Amplifier) and Sony's SXRD™ (Silicon Xtal Reflective Device) technologies. LCoS display technologies provide high contrast and high display resolution, with a high fill factor that minimizes the visibility of the structure evident in traditional transmissive LCD displays.

D-ILA™

JVC introduced D-ILA™ projectors in 2000 for home theatre and fixed installation markets, building on the analog ILA technology it had licensed from Hughes. This technology was also applied to rear projection TV sets in 2004. Although JVC offers 2K D-ILA projectors (the QX-1 supports QXGA inputs) and 4K D-ILA projectors have been demonstrated as part of a consortium funded by the Japan government, these projectors have been limited to a maximum of 8,000 lumens and JVC has not offered a product for the digital cinema market.

SXRD™

In 2003, Sony introduced Silicon Xtal Reflective Display™ (SXRD™) technology in the Qualia HD projector for home theatre markets and followed this with rear-projection HDTV sets in 2005.

Figure 10-1.   D-ILA.

SXRD™ is Sony's patented implementation of LCoS technology. Like D-ILA technology, the organic liquid crystals are vertically aligned for improved contrast. The 4K (4096W*2160H) digital cinema SXRD™ devices have a pixel pitch of 8.5 micron, with 0.35 micron gaps between pixels, on a 1.55″ diagonal imager[1]. Liquid crystal devices are organic components in a liquid dispersion that work by rotating polarized light when a field is applied. One limitation of this polarization technique is that light efficiency is only about 50%.

In late 2005, Sony introduced SXRD™ digital cinema projectors in two models—the SRX-R110 (10,000 lumens) and the SRX-R105 (5,000 lumens). These products use twin Xenon lamps (2kW each for the SRX-R110 model). The SXRD™ projectors are designed to be mounted on a pedestal or table top[2]. The product specifications for each quote a contrast of $>1,800:1$[3] and the projectors are calibrated to gamma 2.6 with the same white point and color primaries as the DCI/SMPTE Reference Projector. Nominally, Digital Cinema Distribution Masters produced on a DLP Cinema® projector should exhibit the same color reproduction on a Sony SXRD™ projector, and vice versa, assuming that each is calibrated properly.

---

1. John Stone and Morgan David, Sony UK Broadcast and Professional Research Labs, "An Integrated System for Digital Cinema Projection and Security", IBC Technical Conference, 2004.
2. http://bssc.sel.sony.com/BroadcastandBusiness/DisplayModel.
3. http://bssc.sel.sony.com/BroadcastandBusiness/DisplayModel.

Figure 10-2. SXRD Device.

Figure 10-3. SXRD Projector.

The Sony SXRD™ 4K projectors can display pictures from a 2K server using the same dual-link SMPTE 372 interfaces as used with the DLP Cinema® projectors, with the projector resizing the 2K images for 4K display. At the time of this writing, there are no DCI-compliant 4K digital cinema servers on the market, and demonstrations of 4K content have involved four quadrant playback from uncompressed post production servers over four dual-link SMPTE 372 (octo-link) interfaces. Sony has announced that they are working on a 4K media block (internal decoder) that is projected to be available before the end of 2006[4].

Sony has also demonstrated prototype GLV™ (Grating Light Valve) projectors on small (less than 20 ft wide) screens in technology showcases in Japan, building on technology it licensed from Silicon Light Machines. Although this technology promises higher contrast, wider color

---

4. Mandel, "Implementation of the First Commercially Available 4K Resolution Projector", SMPTE Conference, 2005.

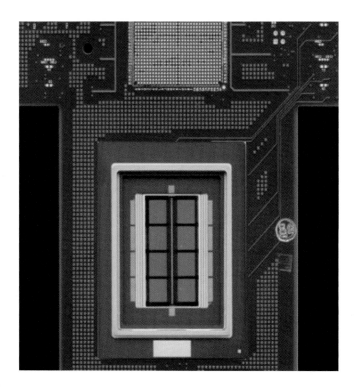

Figure 10-4.   GLV.

gamut, and 4K or higher display resolution, its application to digital cinema display is limited today by the lack of high power solid state lasers as well as potential safety hazards.

CRT Reference Monitors

Reference video monitors play an important role in post production, as the primary display device for telecine transfer, home video mastering, editing, and quality control functions. Traditionally, the professional monitors have been CRT (Cathode Ray Tube) devices, manufactured to higher performance and tighter specifications than consumer displays, but otherwise embodying the same technology as the ubiquitous consumer TV set. CRT technology is over 100 years old, with monochrome displays from the 1910's and color CRTs introduced by RCA in the 1950's. A CRT display is driven by the emission of electrons from the cathode, which are attracted to a high voltage anode. These electrons strike phosphors coated on a glass faceplate, causing the phosphors to emit light. This is an analog system, with the light output related to the signal voltage by a power law expression with a gamma of 2.2. Color CRTs use three electron guns,

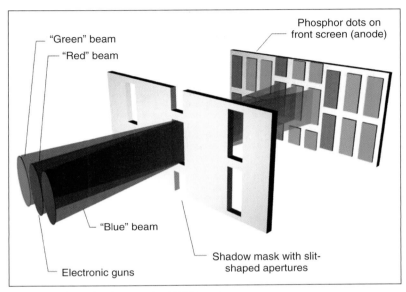

Figure 10-5. Illustration of a Cathode Ray Tube (CRT) imaging system.

a shadow-mask anode, and three color phosphors (red, green and blue). Each electron beam is scanned from left to right and top to bottom, with the odd lines on field one followed by the even lines on field two, creating the familiar television display raster.

Early HDTV sets were also based on CRT technology, but the size of the display was limited to less than 40″ diagonal due to the prohibitive weight of a bigger glass picture tube. The brightness of the display is a function of the spot size of the scanning beam, and since HDTV displays require smaller spots than standard definition displays, this means that HDTV CRTs are dimmer than their (equivalent size) standard definition predecessors. Both of these factors provided a driving force for manufacturers to develop a new display technology capable of bigger, brighter displays to take full advantage of the HDTV signal.

Flat Panel Displays

In the late 1990's, flat panel displays based on plasma technology at sizes of 40″ to 50″ diagonal were introduced to the consumer TV market. Last year, LCD flat panel HDTV displays were introduced in this size range at competitive prices. Meanwhile, rear-projection DLP® and SXRD™ HDTV displays dominate the larger screen size (>50″ diagonal) market. The basic principles behind each of these technologies will be reviewed, along with their strengths and weaknesses, and potential improvements in the near future. Although these technologies have effectively displaced CRT displays in the consumer HDTV market, they all have issues that to date have limited their use as a reference monitor in post production.

Plasma Display Panels

Plasma Display Panels (PDP) are emissive displays, employing a neon-xenon gas mixture that emits ultraviolet (UV) radiation when stimulated by a high voltage discharge. This UV emission in turn stimulates phosphors to emit visible light. This process releases considerable heat and electromagnetic radiation. This basic process is illustrated in Figure 10.6.

Plasma displays are digital in nature—each cell is either on or off, and a grayscale is created by pulse width modulation (PWM) at a high frequency. Plasma displays can be very bright, with a peak white of up to 250 cd/m^2 and a full field white of up to 100 cd/m^2. The real beauty of plasma displays is the low black level since the phosphor can be effectively turned off much like CRTs, supporting a full-field contrast of over 500:1.

The tradeoff is that the native resolution of most high definition plasma displays are 1366 H $\times$ 768 V, compared to the 1920 H $\times$ 1080 V now commonly available with LCD, DLP® and SXRD™ technologies. Power consumption of plasma displays tend to run about 20% higher than same

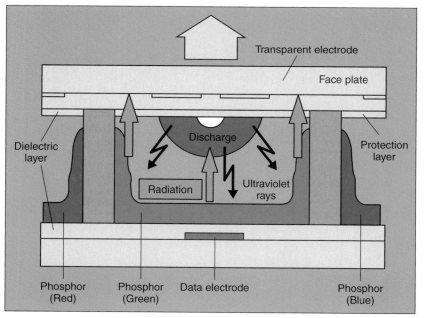

Figure 10-6. Illustration of a plasma imaging cell.

size LCD displays, and plasma displays are heavier. Although the color gamut of plasma displays is typically smaller than Rec. 709 (the standard for professional CRT displays), it is broader than that of typical LCD displays. Figure 10.7 compares the color gamuts of typical plasma and LCD displays to Rec. 709.

Liquid Crystal Displays

Thin Liquid Crystal Displays (LCD) have long been the choice for laptop computers and the technology has matured to the point that it is now cost effective to manufacture LCD panels for consumer TVs of 40″ to 50″ diagonal in size. Liquid crystals act as light shutters, blocking light when the crystals are aligned and passing light when randomly arranged. This effect is known as birefringence. Figure 10.8 illustrates the LCD in operation.

It is now common to find LCD panels with resolution of 1920 H × 1080 V. Typical LCD displays are bright (as high as 500 cd/m²), but deliver a peak contrast of only about 250 : 1, with black levels that are noticeably higher than plasma, DLP® or SXRD™ displays. Typical LCD displays are also impaired by some lag on fast moving objects and a limited viewing angle. Recent improvements in screen compensating films, screen technology and faster LC response times have improved all of these characteristics. In addition, new pulsed LED light sources offer an improved color gamut and virtually eliminate the lag.

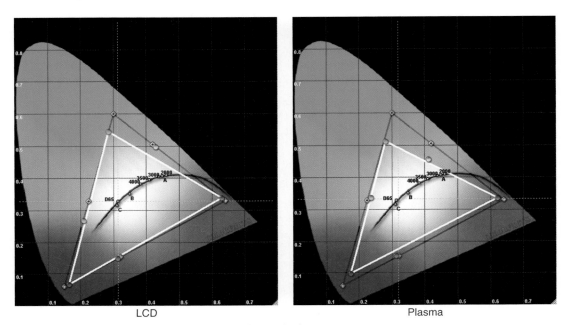

LCD   Plasma

Figure 10-7.   Color gamuts of typical LCD and Plasma displays.

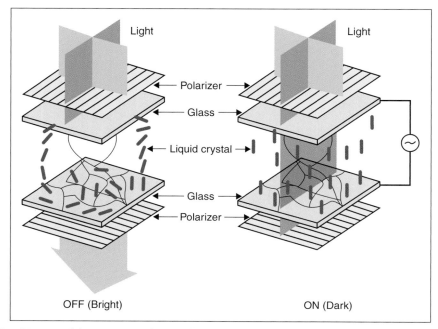

Figure 10-8.   Diagram of the operation of a Liquid Crystal Device (LCD).

High Dynamic Range Displays

High Dynamic Range (HDR) displays have been recently introduced by Brightside[5], using a modulated low resolution LED array as a light source to substantially enhance the contrast of the LCD display. This works on the psychophysical principle that very high contrast cannot be perceived at high spatial frequencies. Studies show that the maximum perceivable local small area contrast is approximately 150:1.

With the modulated LED light source, LCD displays with contrast ratios of over 50,000:1 have been demonstrated, with peak brightness as high as 8500 cd/m². The contrast range of a high dynamic range display implemented in this fashion is effectively the product of each modulation step. Brightside's patented approach convolves the low-resolution LED modulated image with a complementary high-resolution image that drives the LCD display. This image is essentially an edge-enhanced picture with the low frequency components attenuated. This algorithm is also similar in principle to a local tone mapping operator. The bottom line is that it works well, creating smooth high dynamic range pictures with no apparent structure or blockiness.

---

5. Helge Seetzen, et al, "High Dynamic Range Display Systems", ACM Siggraph Conference Proceedings, 2004.

Post Production Applications

Plasma display panels have not been embraced in post production, due to their limited resolution and lack of detail in blacks. LCD displays are widely used in non-critical color applications, including workstations, signal monitoring and editing. However, the traditional CRT is still the technology of choice for color-critical telecine transfers, color grading and quality control. With consumer HDTV sets moving to new technologies, and with several manufacturers discontinuing their professional CRT monitors, it is timely to ask the question, "What technology should replace the CRT as the Reference Monitor for color-critical post production work?" Today, there is no obvious choice that matches the detail in blacks and contrast of the CRT. The use of pulsed LED light sources with LCD displays improves the black detail and increases the contrast, so these techniques may open the door for the use of LCDs as reference monitors in more critical applications.

Digital Cinema color-grading and quality control should be performed with a DLP Cinema® or SXRD™ cinema projector in a mastering room with a screen of 15–20 ft width. Why not use these technologies in rear projection monitors in smaller rooms for dailies transfer, editing or other post production tasks? Rear projection DLP® and SXRD™ HDTV sets are both available in 1080p (1080 V × 1920 H) resolution and exhibit contrast ratios of over 2000:1, with color gamuts that can be calibrated to match Rec. 709. One limitation is the light source, typically UHP lamps that provide a discontinuous spectral output. Today, these sets only offer component analog or DVI/HDMI digital inputs, and support only standard broadcast signal formats, with the signal de-interlaced for 1080/60p display, so there is no way to look at the "raw" signal as you would on a CRT Reference Monitor.

Enhanced Display Technologies

Several technologies provide improvements to digital displays that enhance their picture quality in consumer television applications. Some of these technologies may also be applied to professional monitors.

LED Light Sources

Recently, Texas Instruments published a white paper on the use of LED illumination technology with DLP® HDTV displays[6]. Replacing today's UHP lamps with LED light sources provides several performance advantages including much longer lamp life, instant on, the elimination of color refresh artifacts, dynamically adjustable brightness and extended color gamut. Figure 10.9

---

6. D.J. Segler, "LED TV: Technology Overview and the DLP Advantage", © 2006.

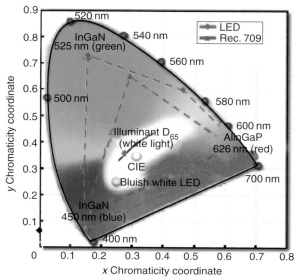

Figure 10-9. Extended gamut with LED illumination.

illustrates the potential color gamut that can be reached with LED illumination, compared to Rec. 709.

Challenges to the implementation of LED light sources include thermal stability and the implementation of fast-switching, high current load drivers. TI utilizes a feedback algorithm to control color shifts, offering superior stability over a wide range of operating temperatures. The rapid switching capability of LED technology is a good match for the fast switching characteristics of DLP® devices. This enables the use of much higher color refresh rates than today's DLP® HDTV designs that employ mechanical color filter wheels. Multiple color segments can be generated and these colors can be randomized, allowing the virtual elimination of color refresh artifacts. Ultimately, images can be created with higher bit depth, better motion fidelity and higher brightness.

Silicon Electro-luminescent Displays

Silicon Electro-luminescent Displays (SED) have been developed and recently demonstrated by Canon and Toshiba. In principle, these displays combine the advantages of emissive phosphors with the solid-state scalability of thin film transistor driving matrices. This should allow 40″ HDTV flat panel displays that match the contrast of CRTs without the brightness tradeoff and prohibitive size and weight. At the time of this writing, SED products have yet to be commercially introduced, but consumer HDTV displays are expected by year end 2007.

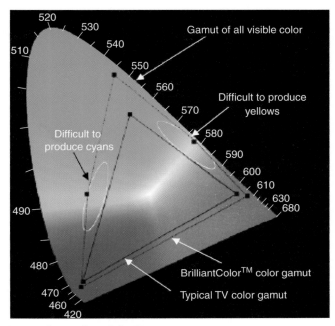

Figure 10-10. Color Gamut of TI's BrilliantColor™ system.

BrilliantColor™

Texas Instruments published a white paper describing their patented BrilliantColor™ technology for enhancing the brightness and color gamut of a DLP® HDTV display[7]. With traditional red, green and blue color primaries, the lamp spectrum is typically split into the same three color bands. Since the spectrum is filtered to create these color bands, substantial light is lost in the regions between the red, green and blue bands. These regions correspond to yellow and cyan. By adding additional yellow and cyan color filters to the wheel, it is possible to recapture as much as 50% more luminance, substantially increasing the brightness of the resulting display.

This technique also enables a much broader color gamut. As described before, the color gamut of a traditional additive display is contained within the triangle formed by the chromaticity coordinates of the three red, green and blue primaries. This system can display any color that is a simple combination of the three primaries. However, it does not allow the display to reproduce certain vivid yellows and cyans that occur naturally. Adding additional yellow and cyan color segments to the color wheel expands the triangle into a wider polygon that encompasses deeper yellows and cyans. Figure 10.10

---

7. David Hutchinson, "Introducing BrilliantColor™ Technology", © 2004.

shows the color gamut of a five primary BrilliantColor™ display system compared to the standard three primary TV system.

In practice, most of today's DLP® HDTV display systems incorporate either six or eight color segments to expand the color gamut, increase the brightness and minimize color refresh artifacts.

Dynamic Iris

Many home theatre projectors employ a dynamic iris to enhance the sequential contrast of the picture. This is a mechanical iris that is regulated by average picture level. Effectively, it closes down as a picture fades to black, lowering the black level of the displayed picture. Using this technique, many home theatre projectors provide contrasts of greater than 4000:1.

Conclusion

As the consumer HDTV market continues to explode, display manufacturers are investing in enhancements to LCD and plasma flat panel technologies, as well as new approaches like modulated LED light sources to improve contrast. Rear projection technologies provide cost effective solutions for the bigger screen. At some point, these digital display technologies will be delivered in a professional "studio grade" monitor for post production applications. However, it is not clear that one technology will be the clear winner, replacing the ubiquitous CRT. With substantial differences in display characteristics, and with the consumer market split between several different technologies, it may be necessary to review home video masters on more than one display.

11
Digital 3D Presentation

Stereoscopic pictures, commonly called 3D, have been around for a long time. Binocular vision gives us the capability to perceive depth, with the brain decoding the depth information from the disparity between the images captured by the left and right eye. The first 3D movies were produced over 100 years ago, but they never caught on due to complexities in capturing and displaying stereoscopic pictures. The second wave of stereoscopic movie presentation occurred in the 1950's as moviemakers and exhibitors were seeking a new sensational experience to revitalize sagging attendance at the box office. Movies that exploited the 3D experience, such as "Bwana Devil" in 1952, "House of Wax", and "Kiss Me Kate" played to avid fans. In 1953, 27 movies were released in 3D format, followed in 1954 by 16 movies, but this tailed off to one in 1955. Once again, the format was doomed by the complexity of dual camera rigs and the cost of double prints and dual projectors, each equipped with polarized filters. When a sophisticated movie was finally made in stereo it was too late, and Hitchcock's "Dial M for Murder" was released in flat format.

In the late 1970's, some daring filmmakers, including Steven Spielberg, again explored the 3D medium in horror films, including "Jaws 3D", "Amityville 3D" and "Halloween 3D". This time, they used anaglyph prints or split frame (over/under) prints to reduce the complexity of projecting 3D. The anaglyph process uses color to encode depth, so it can be presented with a single color print and a pair of glasses with red and (complementary) cyan filters. This makes presentation very practical and cost effective, as it uses a standard 35 mm print on a standard projector with a standard screen. The glasses are inexpensive and light. However, it is at best a pseudo-color picture, because the full range of colors is sacrificed, with color serving the primary function of representing depth. This technique was also used by Robert Rodriguez in 2002 for "Spy Kids 3D: Game Over" which generated over $189M internationally, and in 2005 for "Shark Boy and Lava Girl".

In 2004, Warner Brothers decided to release Robert Zemeckis' "The Polar Express" in IMAX 3D. This movie was hugely successful, generating more than $45M revenue internationally on just 77 IMAX screens equipped for 3D presentation. The proprietary IMAX system uses two film strips along with a rotating linearly polarized shutter and a silver screen. The observer wears inexpensive, light-weight passive linearly polarized glasses. "The Polar Express" utilized computer generated animation, so generating a second view from the 3D model did not mean starting from scratch. However, Sony Imageworks and IMAX reviewed every shot, reworking many of them in order to increase depth of field and adjust transparency. This is not a trivial process, and can add as much as several million dollars to the post production budget.

Meanwhile, IMAX has also shown several short 3D movies that were captured with stereo camera rigs. These included James Cameron's "Ghosts of the Abyss" and "Aliens of the Deep". Audiences have responded enthusiastically to the 3D experience, one that many had never seen except in theme park rides, and one that they cannot get at home.

Digital projection technology has many advantages over film in stereoscopic presentation. Two projectors can be aligned closely, corrected geometrically, and the weave inherent in film prints is eliminated. This makes for a more effective and less tiring 3D display. Even more important in terms of practical implementation, today's DLP Cinema® projectors can support the display of two stereo pictures, meaning that a full-color 3D presentation is possible with a single projector.

In 2005, Disney, working with Dolby and Real D, took advantage of this single-projector capability to release "Chicken Little" in digital 3D to 89 screens in the US, Mexico and Canada. In addition to a DLP Cinema® projector from Christie or Barco, each cinema was equipped with a Dolby server configured to support two playback streams, with a Real D Z-Screen™ active circular polarizer placed in front of the projection lens. Each cinema was also equipped with a silver screen, since the image polarization must be maintained to the observer. This allowed Disney to use relatively inexpensive passive glasses, which were supplied as souvenirs to their patrons. The digital 3D presentation of "Chicken Little" was very successful, generating more than twice the revenue per screen as the standard 2D presentation of the film. Furthermore, the 3D experience generated rave reviews from both critics and satisfied customers.

Before we describe how stereoscopic presentations are presented digitally, let's step back and review the principles of stereoscopic imaging. Depth perception is based on the discrepancy between the image that we see with our left and right eyes, and the brain's interpretation of this

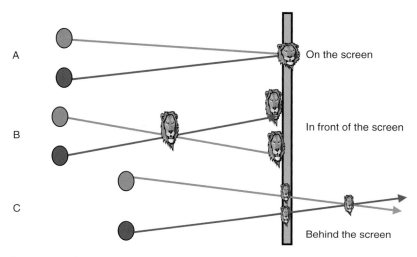

A — On the screen

B — In front of the screen

C — Behind the screen

Figure 11-1.   Stereoscopic Presentation.

parallax effect as depth. When these two images match, as shown in Figure 11.1A[1], the image appears on the plane of the screen. When the image seen by the right eye shifts to the left, and the image seen by the left eye shifts to the right by the same distance, the observer's eyes converge slightly as if tracking an object in front of the screen. This is illustrated in Figure 11.1B. Comfortably viewed 3D images will never make the eyes diverge. An offset of 2.5 inches at the screen plane puts the object at infinity. This is shown in Figure 11.1C.

So what makes a good 3D presentation? For depth to appear natural it is important that it be presented clearly and consistently, with no conflicting cues that remove the observer from the experience. For a comfortable movie experience, this must be maintained for 90 minutes or more. Image registration is critical, in both the original photography and in the projection of the picture. Mis-registration reduces the depth effect and forces the brain to work harder to try to align the disparate images. The unsteadiness of two projected film prints, while not immediately obvious to an observer wearing stereo glasses, can result in fatigue, headaches and even sickness when viewed too long. Some observers are more sensitive than others to this effect.

Stereoscopic pictures impose constraints on cinematography and editing as well. On the capture side, the stereo camera rig places the two cameras side by side, as closely together as the lenses permit, and ideally with the two lenses positioned at the average inter-ocular distance of

1. M. Cowan and L. Nielsen, "3D - How do they do it?", Presentation to IBC, Entertainment Technology Consultants, September 12, 2005.

2.5 inches. This may require the use of a folding mirror which cuts the light in half. For subjects at a distance, where essentially the focal length is infinity, the two lenses are aligned in parallel. For subjects that are closer to the camera, the two lenses must be dove-tailed inward, with the angle adjusted according to the distance between the subject and the camera. If the subject is moving towards the camera, the lenses must be adjusted dynamically to track the subject. Practical close-ups are limited to about 10 feet.

In order to minimize fatigue, it is critical that cuts from one shot to another maintain the 3D plane. Otherwise, the brain is constantly chasing and trying to compensate for changing parallax. This imposes a big restriction on the editor's cuts from close-ups to wide shots, but can be mitigated somewhat through zooms or fades.

The 3D experience can also be damaged by ghosting artifacts or cross-talk between the two eyes. Linear polarization systems rely on angle of view, so they are very sensitive to head angle. The observer needs to keep his head level with the screen, or the picture pulls apart into two disparate views. In the extreme, when viewed at 45 degrees, both eyes see a 50/50 composite of the two views. When an active mechanism is used, such as shuttered glasses or a shuttered Z-screen™ in front of the projection lens, it is critical that the extinction ratio between the two eyes be at least (100:1). Otherwise, a smearing effect is evident on high contrast edges.

Single projector displays interleave the image sequences for the left and right eyes. Therefore, the left and right eyes are out of phase with one another, introducing a judder that makes it harder for the brain to fuse the two views. Full motion fusion occurs at aggregate frame rates above 120 FPS, which can be accomplished by interleaving two 60p video sources, by "double-flashing" or frame doubling two 30p video sources, or by "triple-flashing" two 24p film sources. The latter results in an aggregate frame rate of 144 FPS, which is more than necessary, but perceptibly much smoother than the alternative of "double-flashing" to only 96 FPS. This effect is most evident on high contrast moving graphics or animation, and can be substantially mitigated with even a moderate amount of motion blur.

The size and weight of the stereoscopic glasses also play an important role in the comfort of the viewing experience. Liquid crystal elements and their supporting circuitry and batteries have made shuttered glasses bulkier and heavier than passively polarized glasses. Recent innovations from NuVision™ promise to reduce the weight of shuttered glasses. And finally, one of the big challenges in single-projector presentation is providing adequate brightness on a big screen. Because the single projector systems rely on polarization to separate the two image streams, their efficiency is halved not only by the 50% duty cycle but also by the 50% polarization loss, for a net efficiency of 25%. Due to blanking requirements and optical inefficiencies, the practical performance is only about 15%. This means that a single 3D projector requires nearly 6 times as much light as a traditional (2D) presentation if it were to operate at the same perceived brightness level. Since there are practical limits to lamp power, this means either reducing the size of the 3D image or accepting a lower effective light level (to the eyes of the observer) for 3D presentation. In practice, this usually means equipping the projector with the biggest lamp available, limiting the screen size to 40 ft wide or so, and accepting a light level of 3–5 ft L at the observer's eyes. This is running at nearly one third the level of a standard 2D presentation, so the picture must be graded accordingly. These issues will be discussed in more detail later in this chapter.

Light Levels for 3D

As a baseline, let's examine the dual projector solution that is typically used for theme park and special venue 3D presentation. Each projector is equipped with a linear polarizer, one horizontally oriented and the other vertically oriented. A silver screen is required to maintain polarization to the observer, who wears inexpensive passive glasses with complementary linear polarizing filters to separate the two pictures. This system produces minimal crosstalk when the glasses are level with the screen, but ghosting begins to appear with even a small head tilt of a few degrees (ghosting is 1% at 6 degrees of tilt). The strength of this system is its light output. For two 20,000 lumen projectors, Figure 11.2 shows the system components and the net luminance of 15,000 lumens (to the eye)[2].

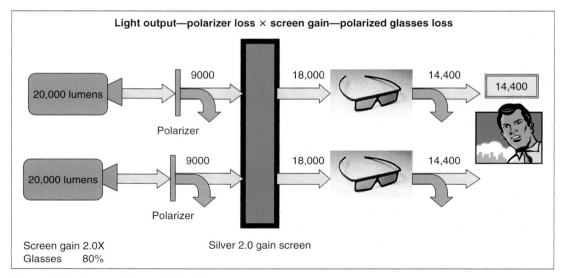

Figure 11-2. Passive Polarized Light Efficiency.

---

2. Ibid.

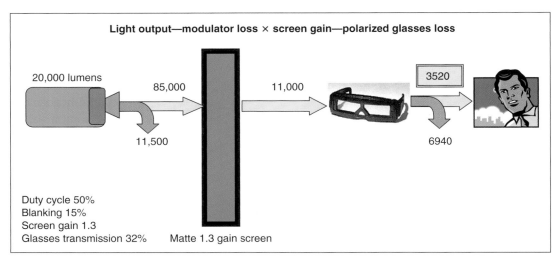

Figure 11-3.   One Projector Active Glasses Light Efficiency.

The silver screen is an important part of this; for this comparison a gain of 2.0 is assumed. Even higher gain silver screens are available, but with a substantial tradeoff in angle of view.

Next, let's look at a single projector stereographic presentation with active shuttered glasses. The advantage of this approach is that it can be used with a standard matte screen. A custom silver screen does not have to be installed. The downside is that the active glasses are relatively expensive (NuVision™ has just announced cinema glasses at $25 per pair) and must be collected, cleaned and reused by the exhibitor. This approach has light losses due to duty cycle, blanking period, lower gain matte screen and the efficiency of the LCD glasses. A typical screen gain of 1.3X is assumed for the matte screen. For one 20,000 lumen projector, Figure 11.3 shows the component losses and the net luminance of 3500 lumens to the eye[3].

Real D's proprietary Z-Screen™ combines the two approaches. In this case the Z-Screen™ active polarizer is placed in front of the projection lens (see Figure 11.4), which means that the glasses can be relatively inexpensive passive glasses. It uses a circular polarization technique, however, rather than simple linear polarization, so the thin film coatings used to fabricate the glasses are more expensive than the traditional linear polarizers. However, these glasses can be manufactured in quantity for under $1 per pair, making them effectively a souvenir item. This approach does require a silver screen to maintain the image polarization to the observer.

---

3. Ibid.

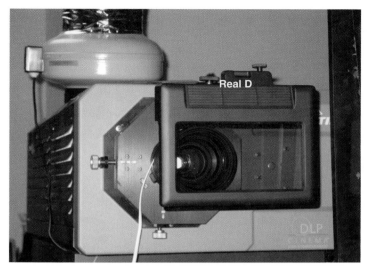

Figure 11-4. Real D Z-Screen™.

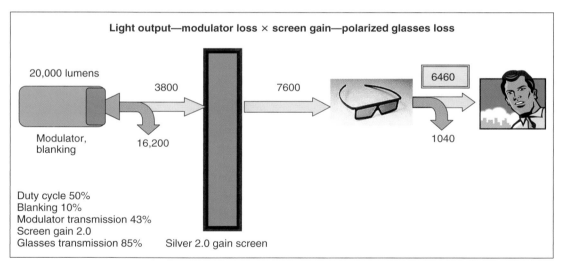

Figure 11-5. One Projector Passive Stereo Light Efficiency.

The Real D approach gets some extra brightness from the higher screen gain, but requires the installation of a silver screen. The Z-Screen™ modulator reduces the light, along with the blanking interval and some absorption in the passive glasses. For a 20,000 lumen projector, Figure 11.5 shows that a net luminance of 6500 lumens to the eye can be achieved.[4]

4. Ibid.

For completeness, there is another approach that divides the color spectrum into six bands, two each for red, green and blue. So, unlike the anaglyph approach, it can reproduce a full color image. Daimler Benz's proprietary Infitec™ color filters are placed over the projection lens and complementary band-pass filters are employed in the glasses. This approach uses a standard matte screen. The glasses require narrow-band coatings that are relatively expensive at this time ($50 per pair), but the price could come down substantially in volume. At the time of this writing, the Infitec™ system has been used in single-chip projection systems employing a 6-element filter wheel for design workstations and small projection screens, or in dual-projector configurations for special venues, but has never been deployed in a cinema presentation. The proponents of this system claim higher efficiency than shuttered glasses, more tolerance of head angle than linear polarizers, and compatibility with standard matte screens. This system is illustrated in Figure 11.6[5].

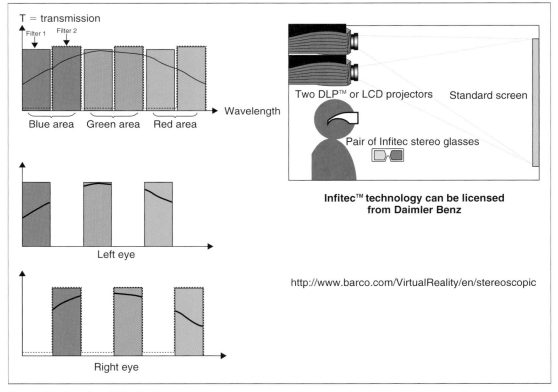

Figure 11-6.   Infitec™ Color Filters.

5. http://www.barco.com/VirtualReality/en/stereoscopic/infitec.asp

	Display Option	Efficiency	Brightness with 45 ft W Screen*
Single Projector	Active Glasses Standard Screen (1.3X)	18%	3.5 ft L
	Z-Screen™ Silver Screen (2.0X)	32%	6 ft L
Dual Projectors	Linear Polarizers Silver Screen (2.0X)	38%	14 ft L
	Infitec Color Filters Standard Screen (1.3X)	27%	6.5 ft L
* 20,000 lumen projector			

Table 11-A. Comparison of Light Efficiency.

With two 20,000 lumen projectors equipped with Infitec™ filters, and using the manufacturer's specifications, it is estimated that a net luminance of 5000 lumens can be achieved.

The relative light levels of these four approaches are compared in Table 11-A, using a 45 foot wide screen. The gain of the silver screens is assumed to be 2.0 and that of the matte screen is assumed to be 1.3. In all cases, the projectors are assumed to have 20,000 lumen output. The single projector solutions are capable of delivering a net brightness of 3.5–6 ft L to the eyes of the observer, while the dual linearly polarized projector solution can deliver 14 ft L to the observers' eyes, equivalent to the presentation light levels for standard 2D presentations. The dual-projector Infitec™ solution delivers 6.5 ft L to the eyes of the observer.

SMPTE DC28 has just formed a working group, DC28.40, to develop standards and recommended practices for stereoscopic distribution and exhibition. One of the key issues is light level. Because of the inefficiencies of the various presentation approaches described earlier, and the interest in using single projector solutions for cost reasons, there is tremendous pressure to make 3D presentation work at lower light levels than the standard 14 ft L for 2D presentation. Disney and Dolby agreed to a target of 5 ft L for their "Chicken Little" installations, and accepted light levels as low as 3.5–4 ft L. This worked well, and no customers complained about dim pictures. Many would argue that 3D pictures look even better at higher light levels, and indeed they do. But they still look great at 5 ft L, and it offers audiences a whole new experience that is commercially compelling.

If a lower light level is standardized for 3D presentation, let's say at 5 ft L, it becomes critical that this light level, and representative polarizers and glasses, are used for color-grading and quality control operations in creating the master for distribution. There is little precedence in this area. "Chicken Little" was mastered at 3.5 ft L (at the eye), and approved for presentation between 3.2 and 5.5 ft L. The premiere was shown at 5 ft L.

However, this also means that the master cannot be presented in 2D without a compensating light level adjustment of the projector; otherwise the picture will appear much too bright. This is important because it is desirable to have one distribution master that plays on both 3D and 2D screens for two reasons. Firstly, not all screens will be equipped for 3D and secondly, a 2D presentation is better than none at all, if some part of the 3D presentation system were to fail.

One way to make the 2D presentation look like the 3D master would be to turn down the brightness of the 2D projector by substituting a smaller lamp or adding a ND filter. Although consistent with the artistic vision of the 3D master, this would impair the contrast of the resulting picture, "dumbing it down" to make it match the light level constraints of 3D presentation. It is possible that a global correction could be applied in the projector 1-D or 3-D look-up tables for displaying a 3D master on a projector configured for 2D presentation, perhaps trading some but not all light for a decrease in color saturation. More experimentation is necessary to understand if a global correction is effective and robust. If it works, the compensating color setup could be implemented easily with a second Projector Configuration File (PCF) for 2D presentation.

Of course, supporting a single distribution master for both 3D and 2D dictates that the stereo track files are separate, one for the left eye and a second for the right, and that a playlist be constructed that either delivers dual streams for 3D presentation or a single stream for 2D presentation. Likewise, the server would need to communicate to the projector whether it was to select the interleaved dual-link inputs for 3D presentation or the standard link configuration for 2D mode.

Dual-link Inputs for 3D

It was described earlier how a single DLP Cinema® projector can accept two input streams, one for each of the left and right eyes, and interleave and replicate them for display. This has been accomplished initially with servers that encoded the data as 4:2:2 sub-sampled YC_bC_r, allowing each channel to be delivered over a single SMPTE 292M link. Since standard projectors have dual-link inputs, one link can be assigned to each input channel.

Although the DCI specification requires full color sampling (4:4:4) at 12 bits per channel for storage and delivery of standard (2D) pictures to the projector, it does provide an exception that supports 4:2:2 color sub-sampling for 48 FPS mode. It does not call out 3D specifically here or anywhere else in the specification, but two 24 FPS streams together add up to 48 FPS. So, by extending the initial practice of two 4:2:2 10-bit YC_bC_r streams delivered over two links, the same approach can be applied to the XYZ data.

Within the JPEG2000 standard color encoding, an Irreversible Color Transform (ICT) is applied to the independent color channels to de-correlate these channels and reduce the overall bit rate requirements. On playback, an Inverse ICT is applied to reconstruct the signal for output to the display. The ICT and Inverse ICT are simple 3x3 matrices that are specified by ITU Rec. 601 for conversion from RGB to YC_bC_r and back, and are applied to the gamma space signals. Although these transforms are not optimized for use with XYZ input data, initial testing has shown that they work well, reducing the bit rate requirements for artifact-free compression by approximately 50%.[6] So, if the Inverse ICT is turned off in the decoder, a simple mode to implement in the commonly used ADI chip set, then the server can deliver two 4:2:2 sub-sampled YC_xC_z color streams to the projector. The projector can apply the inverse ICT in its input color space conversion matrix, since this matrix is applied in gamma-space. Initial testing has shown that this approach works reasonably well, but more testing is needed to verify that it works robustly without generating contouring artifacts with a full range of image content.

3D IN THE HOME

3D display is available for home video and games, but content availability has limited this to a niche market. Of course the production of 3D movies will bolster the supply of content.

Sensio (Montreal, Canada) offers a proprietary encoding format that is DVD compatible. The left and right channels of each frame are squeezed into a single video frame. Upon playback from a special Sensio-equipped DVD player, or from a Sensio external video signal processor, the two channels are interleaved to support a 60 FPS output. The observers wear shuttered glasses that are synchronized with the IR vertical sync output of the Sensio box. It works with any video projector or television display that is equipped with VGA inputs. Although this technique works surprisingly well, it is impaired somewhat by visible flicker (60 FPS is below the flicker threshold for interleaved 3D images), and reduced horizontal resolution due to the anamorphic squeeze applied for DVD-compatible storage. Sensio offers several IMAX 3D films and a limited number of 3D movies in its library.

DDD provides a custom Tri-Def DVD software player that generates auto-stereoscopic 3D output from standard DVDs. Auto-stereoscopic viewing means that no glasses are required. An N-Video GeForce or similar graphics card is required. This technique places the left eye and right eye views into interleaved vertical columns. DDD has a custom algorithm that uses the motion differences between video fields to create a depth effect. Combined with lenticular LCD displays from Sharp or Stereographics, it works reasonably well on content with motion, although the 3D effect is content sensitive. Although this technique works with any interlaced video source, the horizontal resolution

6. W. Husak, Dolby, "Bit-Rate Requirements for JP2K Encoding", SMPTE 2004.

of the display is halved by the process. It is also very sensitive to viewing position – there is a very narrow sweet spot.

NHK demonstrated 3D-HD at NAB 2006, using MPEG-TS to encode the left and right views squeezed into a single HDTV frame. A customized HD-DVD player output the two views as interleaved 1080/60i video fields through a standard HDMI interface. Micropol™ screens were placed over 1080/60i LCD flat panel displays, providing opposing circular polarization on alternating lines. The viewer wears inexpensive passive glasses. Although this technique reduces both horizontal and vertical resolution by a factor of two, it is compatible with the broadcast channel, the consumer media format and the secure HDMI consumer interface, and the pictures are surprising good when viewed at a normal viewing distance.

Games provide another ready source of 3D images. Since games are based on underlying 3D models, it is possible to generate two stereo views from these models. The Microsoft 360 game console supports stereo outputs in its 720/60p format. Again, it must be viewed with shuttered glasses, synchronized with an IR emitter.

Lightspeed Design, working with InFocus, has introduced a custom DLP home theatre projector, the InFocus DepthQ™ stereoscopic projector. The advantage of this display is that it runs at 120 FPS, creating a frame interleaved 3D sequence that is above the flicker frequency. It must be coupled with 3D playback software from Lightspeed.

12
The Future

Digital Cinema mastering and exhibition are new processes based on standards and business models that intend to enhance the business of distribution and exhibition companies, while preserving the interests of the creative community. But digital technology may also be disruptive, because it opens up new possibilities, such as the delivery and presentation of alternative content including live events. It is always dangerous to speculate on what the future may hold as the adoption of digital cinema is just beginning and the process will take time. This chapter will discuss some of the opportunities for enhancements to the digital cinema process or presentation, some of which are practical today, others which may be feasible in the next decade, and some of which may never be adopted.

It is no longer a question of whether digital cinema will be adopted—the conversion has already begun—but it is still hard to predict how quickly and how completely it will occur. Will film distribution and presentation ever be phased out? Will all of today's cinemas convert to digital, or will some of them shut down? Opinions vary widely, even among those groups with common interests like distributors and exhibitors.

Now that standards have been established and the major studios have committed to making all of their movies available for digital distribution, two key issues have been resolved. With third party financing available and business models based on virtual print fees developed, neither exhibitors nor distributors must make up front investments. The capital costs are paid by the studios as they book movies on digital screens. This is simply a substitution cost for traditional film prints. But the studios don't save much money until lots of digital screens are installed and the leases paid down, and the exhibitors don't get the full benefits of promotion or cost savings until they have fully converted. With push from the studios, and pull from exhibitors who won't want to fall behind, it is likely that the demand for rapid conversion will grow.

Initially, the deployment of digital cinema systems will be paced by the capacity of system integrators to install and service the systems. Since the market has been nascent while the standards and business models were being sorted out, manufacturers and system integrators have built up minimal capacity. However, the capacity is not likely to be limited on the manufacturing side, once long lead items such as lenses are procured. In 2006, the collective supply capacity with four projector manufacturers and six server manufacturers providing DCI-compliant equipment is estimated to be 2000 to 4000 systems per year, but this can easily be doubled or tripled as the demand materializes.

A bigger issue is the infrastructure for field installations and service support. Installation in the cinema environment and integration with legacy audio and theatre automation systems is not a trivial task and current cinema service technicians need to be re-trained to support digital technologies. The same field installation teams will also make on-site service calls. In order to provide cost-effective maintenance, the leading system integrators are implementing network operational centers with remote monitoring capabilities for all installed equipment. This allows them to track critical operational parameters and even take corrective action before equipment fails. It also allows them to troubleshoot problems quickly and cost effectively. They are also making provisions for regional parts depots and overnight delivery and swap-out of modular subsystems. But, hiring and training the field installation teams will take some time, and this is likely to constrain installations to 2000 or less in 2006. However, the collective capacity in the industry will ramp up rapidly, with ample resources available within 2–3 years.

Since the total world-wide cinema market is at most 150,000 screens and is growing at less than 5% annually, it is not likely that this market will attract many new entrants and there may even be some consolidation. And there is little incentive for manufacturers, system integrators or service providers to staff up for a rapid deployment, since the market is capped. The most likely scenario is that the deployment will follow an annual doubling profile, starting with 2000 in 2006 and 4000 in 2007, eventually capping at about 8000–10,000 new screens per year. With this scenario, it would take 5–6 years to convert the entire US market, although that would not leave any extra capacity for worldwide deployment.

A more likely scenario is that digital cinema deployments will precede in parallel around the world, at least in developed markets in Europe and Asia. It is likely to take at least 10 years to convert the 75,000 or so screens worldwide that receive first run Hollywood films. So what will happen to the remaining 75,000 screens in the world? Will they convert to DCI-compliant digital cinema systems? Or will they settle for lower cost (and lower performance) systems? This one is harder to predict. Costs of DCI-compliant systems will come down by as much as 50% or more as scale economies are achieved. This may be enough to open up the larger market. However, many of these screens are in regions of the world (China and India, for example) that do not depend on Hollywood content today and do not generate nearly as much revenue per screen. One possibility is that a lower-cost, "E-Cinema" standard may be deployed in regions that do not depend on Hollywood content. Such a system could be based on HD-MPEG2 and utilize lower brightness, lower cost projectors.

Meanwhile, alternative entertainment channels will provide increasing competition for the cinema experience. Most experts predict the number of cinema screens to plateau or even decline slightly. Weighing all these factors, my prognosis is that approximately 100,000 worldwide screens will convert to DCI-compliant digital cinema systems within 10 to 15 years, and that of the remaining screens, maybe half will convert to lower cost E-Cinema systems, and half will shut down. I also predict that the major studios will discontinue their distribution of film prints within the same time period, perhaps hastening the final conversion at some point by levying an extra print charge on exhibitors who haven't yet converted to digital. Considering all these factors, the predicted conversion of the cinema market from film to digital technology is illustrated in Figure 12.1.

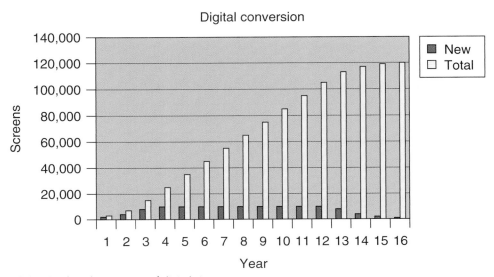

Figure 12-1. Predicted conversion of digital cinema screens.

Alternative Content

Digital cinema technology also enables alternative (non-movie) uses of the cinema. Early experiments with special event bookings in cinemas have had mixed results, with the most successful alternative content being concerts with well-known musicians such as "The Rolling Stones Live from Rio" delivered through National Cinemedia's Big Screen Concert program, and sporting events that are not otherwise available on local television, such as "Worldwide Wrestling Federation" shown on Cineplex Odeon screens in Canada. The biggest challenge has been marketing and publicizing the events and getting patrons used to the concept of going to the cinema for something other than movies. If booked on Monday or Tuesday nights, typically weak nights for movie attendance, these special events can generate larger revenues.

Alternative content is available in HDTV broadcast format, and most likely will be MPEG2 encoded. In order to support this format, in addition to the digital cinema distribution master (DCDM), it is useful for digital cinema equipment to provide an additional operating mode. For servers, this means support for HD-MPEG2 decoding for packaged content in addition to JPEG 2000. For live broadcasts, the signal may be decoded by the HD satellite receiver and delivered directly to the projector, or passed through the server.

For projectors, supporting HDTV inputs means setting up for 1080/60i or 720/60p inputs and ITU Rec. 709 color space. An external de-interlacer, or an optional plug-in de-interlacing card, may be required for 1080/60i sources, with this box providing either HD-SDI or DVI inputs to the projector. Since the HDTV pictures will be magnified on the big screen, compression artifacts at 19 Mbps may be apparent. A video processing box such as the Teranex Mini™ may be required to clean up the signal and remove blocking artifacts.

Cinemas may also be booked during non-operating hours such as week-day mornings for private parties or business events. In these cases, other video inputs may be required including VGA graphics for business presentations, DVI inputs from consumer DVD players, and component video inputs from video game consoles. These signals may also require an external conversion box.

Impact of Wider Gamut Light Sources

As discussed before, today's projectors have Xenon light sources. Laser Light Engines and other companies are developing light sources based on solid state lasers. Today, these lasers do not provide enough power to light up a big screen, but advances in efficiency of individual lasers as well as bundling for higher light output may make lasers a feasible alternative within 5–10 years. Why lasers? The biggest driving force is extended life compared to high power Xenon lamps and

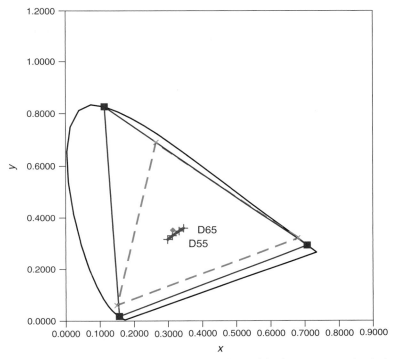

Figure 12-2. The potential color gamut of a laser projector is shown (blue line), compared with the color gamut of the Digital Cinema Reference Projector with a Xenon light source (dashed red line).

the potential to reduce the operating cost. A 5 kW Xenon lamp costs approximately $2000 and must be replaced approximately twice a year.

Lasers also offer a wider color gamut and enhanced contrast. Figure 12.2 shows an example of possible laser primaries from Laser Light Engines[1], and the resulting color gamut compared to today's Xenon-based digital cinema projectors. Potentially, a laser illumination system could be applied to either DLP or LCOS projection systems. In addition, lasers are required for the Grating Light Valve (GLV) technology that Sony purchased from Silicon Light Machines and is in the process of commercializing. However, there are some downsides to laser illumination that must be considered. One obvious issue is safety—laser projection systems must contain failsafe switches that prevent scanning mechanisms such as GLV from stalling and projecting a blinding laser beam. Using spatial modulators like DLP or LCOS chips is a much safer approach, as the laser power is dispersed over the whole screen.

---

1. Dr. Peter F. Moulton, Q-Peak, a wholly owned subsidiary of Physical Sciences, Inc

Another issue with narrow-band laser illumination that goes with its wider color gamut is that a laser light source will increase the differences between perceived colors from one observer to another. Broad-band light sources like Xenon are much more forgiving of variations in the color responses between observers. This sensitivity can be minimized somewhat by bundling multiple laser wavelengths to spread the spectrum, but with a corresponding reduction of the color gamut.

Another option is to create a multi-primary display, for example, using six primaries to reconstruct the color rather than the traditional red, green and blue. This could be used to widen the color gamut in the subtractive colors, particularly cyan where today's digital cinema projectors fall short of film. Note that a six primary display does not require that the color be encoded in six channels. Color can still be represented in a wide gamut XYZ color space, and then converted to a six-primary display system by mixing color channels within the projector. This is similar to the P7v2 color processing in DLP Cinema® projectors that was described in Chapter 9.

A projector with a laser light source and a wider color gamut is likely to see use first in the mastering environment. This supports the creation of wider gamut (and higher contrast) masters. And XYZ color space can record these wider color gamuts. The challenge comes with backward compatibility with today's projectors. Wide gamut masters will need to be gamut-mapped so that they can be displayed on today's Xenon projectors without introducing clipping artifacts. An approach to gamut mapping was described in Chapter 8. This gamut mapping operation is a reproduction task that is projector specific, if the requirement of one distribution master is maintained. So this means that today's projectors must be built with a gamut mapping capability inside, or with provision to add the gamut mapping capability in the future.

Digital Cinematography

Cinematography is the last part of the filmmaking process to embrace digital technology. Traditional video cameras, although enabled with CCD image sensors and digital image processing in the 1990's, do not offer the dynamic range of film, imposing restrictions on the production process and limiting creative flexibility in post production. This is explored in Chapter 2. In 2005, several film-style digital cameras were introduced by Panavision and Arri, the two leading manufacturers of 35 mm motion picture film cameras, and by Dalsa, a new entrant in the market. These complement the Thomson Viper that was introduced in 2003. All of these cameras have sufficient resolution (2K or greater) to produce high quality masters for film or digital distribution.

Although these cameras have different sensors and different architectures, they share a common approach to capturing extended dynamic range images with a film-sized, single chip sensor that allows the use of standard 35 mm film lenses. For the first time, film cinematographers have access to digital cameras that look and feel like film cameras and provide the flexibility to fit into

Figure 12-3. Photograph of an Arriflex D-20 Digital Camera.

the traditional filmmaking process. Michael Mann's "Collateral" (2004) was shot primarily with the Thomson Viper and Sony F900 digital cameras, but still relied on film for some scenes. Warner Brothers' "Superman Returns" was shot entirely with the Panavision Genesis digital camera and has a Summer 2006 release date.

At the time of this writing, most experienced cinematographers still prefer the characteristics of film origination, but many are beginning to experiment with the new film-style digital cameras. Although these cameras have some limitations today, it is expected that these limitations will be addressed promptly and that the convenience of direct digital dailies and streamlined post production will make digital origination a compelling option within the next 5 years or so.

These cameras are also capable of capturing an extended color gamut, when compared to traditional television cameras designed to ITU Rec. 709. Although the manufacturers do not publish the spectral responses or the effective color primaries of these cameras, it is a straightforward matter to characterize a calibrated camera and to compute a 3×3 matrix to convert from the cameras native RGB color components to scene-referred XYZ for digital cinema.

Digital mastering will still involve a creative color grading step, just as it does today with film origination, and this operation will most likely be performed in the camera's native RGB space, with the colorist looking at the results on a calibrated digital cinema Reference Projector. If the digital camera material is being inter-cut with film scenes, it may be desirable to encode the channels into printing density format for compatibility with film. The color corrected master has output-referred color, and the encoding to XYZ is simply a linearization, followed by a 3×3 matrix that is computed from the white point and color primaries of the Reference Projector, as described in Chapter 7.

ACADEMY INTERCHANGE FILE FORMAT

At the time of this writing, the Scientific and Technical Council of the Academy of Motion Picture Arts and Sciences (AMPAS) has sponsored an industry-wide project to try to define a common file format for interchanging digital images between post production facilities. This extended range file format is intended as an input to visual effects work as well as digital color grading. It may also be used to represent the final color-corrected output, such as that contained in the DCDM.

There are two common workflows in motion picture digital post production today. Today, most digital intermediate processes involve the conforming and color-grading of digitized film in RGB printing density space, which has a logarithmic characteristic. However, most computer graphics animation and visual effects compositing is rendered in a linear space. Industrial Light and Magic (ILM) has offered the use of its open source Open EXR (extended range) file format which encodes extended dynamic range information as 16-bit floating point numbers for each RGB color channel. Most film scanners and color correctors for digital intermediate use the DPX or Cineon file format which uses 10-bit log-encoded integer numbers for each RGB color channel. At first look, these two approaches are incompatible and proponents of each are not willing to revamp their entire workflow.

An emerging solution is to transform the film printing density information into Linearized Printing Density, or LPD, where the logarithmic data is linearized using a nominal film transform. This LPD data can then be stored in Open EXR file format, along with colorimetric information representing the white point and color primaries of the film system. The key is defining a simple transform from film to LPD and back, so that Open EXR can be used for file interchange, but facilities can import and process data in printing density space if they so desire.

Some have proposed a complete "un-building" of the film into a linear scene-referred representation. This is problematic for several reasons. First, a true un-building process would require detailed characterization of each film emulsion, information that film manufacturers consider confidential. Second, an inverse linearization of the film's characteristic curve would introduce very high gains in the non-linear toe and shoulder, which could introduce artifacts. And finally, cinematographers often select one film emulsion over another because they like its specific color reproduction characteristics, so to remove this personality from the image is perhaps going too far.

At the time of this writing, work continues to define the color transformations. Tests will be conducted to verify the transforms and the practicality and transparency of implementing these conversions as part of the film reading operation. Assuming this proves feasible, sample source code will be provided to allow software vendors to implement compatible readers and writers. And finally, the Academy intends to submit the results of their consensus file format to SMPTE for formal standardization.

Enhanced Motion

The DCI Specification supports 48 FPS motion capture for smoother motion rendition without the judder associated with 24 FPS capture. This has been demonstrated with today's DLP Cinema® projectors using two interleaved streams, one containing odd and the other even frames. Indeed, the picture is much cleaner and smoother when shots involve fast moving subjects or camera pans. It is not likely that 48 FPS cinematography will be used with film origination because it doubles the raw stock and lab costs. However, with the adoption of digital cinematography this may become more practical, since the tape (or alternative digital storage) costs are minimal.

If a digital cinema master is produced at 48 FPS, one must also consider backward compatibility with 24 FPS film release. One cannot simply drop odd frames, because although the motion rate would be consistent, the result would be enhanced judder because each of these pictures were captured with an effective 25% aperture function, rather than the 50% aperture function typically used with film origination. This substantially reduces the motion blur creating sharper individual frames that will judder with motion. It is necessary to average frames, effectively recreating the 50% aperture function to make it look like typical 24 FPS origination.

Digital Cinema-Centric Workflow

As described in Chapter 6, today's digital intermediate processes are typically implemented in a film-centric way, with a RGB printing density representation used as the working color space. As digital cinema distribution becomes the primary medium, and as digital cinematography becomes more prevalent, it is likely that these processes will shift to a digital cinema-centric workflow. This means that color correctors will likely be reconfigured to work on linear RGB data in Open EXR file format, and that this data will be displayed directly on the Reference Projector without a 3D LUT for print film emulation. It is then a simple step to transform the color-corrected linear data into the XYZ 12-bit integer color data for the DCDM.

In this workflow, it is necessary to build an inverse print film color transformation (3D color LUT) that translates the Digital Cinema Distribution Master into printing density for the film output process. This process is already used today by ILM and Pixar, who treat their digital pictures as the primary medium, and the film output as a secondary deliverable.

Color Appearance Models

Mark Fairchild and others have published substantial research on color appearance models[2] that essentially create color transforms to compensate for different output devices and viewing conditions. In Chapter 6, the current practice of making a creative color trim pass to compensate for the difference in viewing conditions between home video and cinema display environments was discussed. However, as color appearance models are perfected, it should be possible to automate this trim pass, turning it into a simple rendering pass.

Color appearance models may also be applied to re-rendering color for other viewing environments, for example iPod™ or cell phone displays. This technique could also be applied for compensation for different digital display technologies, but in this case the rendering would need to be implemented in the display since it is device specific. Although impractical today, it will certainly be feasible and cost effective in the not too distant future.

What do you Archive?

As we move from a film to a digital world, the question of what materials to archive is stirring heated debates. The biggest problem is that there is no accepted archival digital medium today, due to both media deterioration and software and hardware obsolescence. The lowest risk approach today to archive the finished digital master is to make black and white film separations that have a proven shelf life of over 100 years (if stored properly) and can always be reconstructed optically or re-digitized. At the time of this writing, the Scientific and Technical Council of AMPAS has a project team investigating options for archiving on digital media.

Element	Analog Process	Digital Process
Original	Original negative (o-neg)	Original tapes
Color corrected master	Timed Inter-positive (IP)	Digital Source Master (DSM)
Reference picture	Answer Print	Digital Cinema Distribution Master (DCDM)
Video master	HD 1080/24p	HD 1080/24p
Long term storage	Black and White Separations	Black and White Separations

Table 12-A. A comparison of archival elements for analog and digital processes.

---

2. Mark D. Fairchild, *Color Appearance Models*, Wiley © 2005

Once we have a digital storage medium, which elements should be saved for the future? With traditional film production, it is common practice to store the original camera negative, a timed IP, and an answer print in addition to the black and white separations. A HD 1080/24p master tape is also stored as the home video master. A similar approach should be taken in the digital world. A comparison of archival elements for film and digital post production is shown in Table 12-A.

The original negative or original digital tapes should be stored. The conformed and graded Digital Source Master (DSM) is the equivalent to the timed IP. It preserves the extended range of the original photography if the movie needs to be re-mastered in the future for a high dynamic range display. The most likely file format here is the Open EXR file format, storing linear RGB data. It is important to tag the data with the color characteristics of the Reference Projector used in mastering, and the 3D color LUT used to emulate print film.

Although the various distribution formats can easily be regenerated from the DSM, it is also worth saving the output Digital Cinema Distribution Master (DCDM) in TIFF-16 file format, storing 12-bit X′Y′Z′ color data, as well as the HD 1080/24p home video master. The DCDM serves as the answer print for color reference in future releases or restorations as well as the master from which additional copies can be made. The HD 1080/24p format is the master from which all other home video formats can be made.

Conclusion

Digital technology is being adopted throughout the whole film-making process. Many of these applications are evolutionary, replacing the traditional analog methods in one part of the process, while complementing the traditional workflow. Complementary applications that were adopted rapidly include non-linear editing, visual F/X and digital sound. Other changes, such as the digital distribution and exhibition of movies have much broader impacts, changing multiple parts of the process simultaneously, and impacting the whole industry. It is easy to view digital cinema as disruptive and risky. But it is also an opportunity to streamline the process and improve the quality of the cinema experience. The creative use of color is a powerful emotive tool. But to be used effectively, this color must be reproduced in a calibrated and consistent fashion on each and every screen. And this is where color science can be applied to support the art of movie-making.

Index